BEHOLD YOUR GOD

Contents

Introduction

'Too wonderful for me', Job. 42. 3; Ps. 139. 6

There can be no subject that would draw from the lips of the believer such a response as a study of the character or attributes of God. As we wade into the shallows with the mighty ocean before us, we are struck by the vastness of the expanse of water. Yet, how pale a picture when compared with the greatness of our God! The depths of the Divine character and Person cannot be fathomed.

The patriarch Job was a very godly man. The opening verse of the book that bears his name indicates that he was 'blameless and upright, and one who feared God and shunned evil', v. 1 NKJV. Apart from the manner of his life, he was also a spiritual man, for he 'rose up early in the morning, and offered burnt offerings according to the number of them all [his children]', v. 5. However, as one that was eventually brought into the dust of personal suffering and loss, Job came to acknowledge that he didn't really know God as he thought he did. All that he had heard and stored up in his mind could not be compared with what he was brought to see. Clearly, his miserable comforters knew even less than Job. Heavy as the burdens of Job's experience may have been, for Job, as for us, there was no substitute for a personal relationship with and experience of God in his life. The darkness of his experiences was compensated by the enjoyment of the light of God's presence.

In contrast with Job, it is suggested that David wrote Psalm 139 alongside the events of 2 Samuel chapter 7. As David considered the situation of the ark and unfolded to Nathan the prophet what was in his heart, he was, in many respects, at the height of his spiritual experience as king. The Lord God, the Lord of hosts, and the God of Israel are the titles used by David as he sat before the Lord in prayer. In his appreciation of his God, David speaks of His omniscience, His sovereignty, His uniqueness, His redemptive power, His purposes in grace, His truthfulness and His goodness. Clearly, David had a significant knowledge of his God and this was far from theoretical. As, like Job in a different context, he had been brought through the trials caused by Saul and his followers, so David had proved his God in the furnace of testing! But David's thoughts of his God also enabled him to remain humble, as he says, 'Who am I, O Lord God? And what is my house, that thou hast brought me hitherto?' v. 18. It is a right appreciation of God that will lead us to a right appreciation of ourselves!

In this book we wish to highlight some of the truths relating to God and to see those truths exemplified in the Person of the Lord Jesus Christ. However,

Behold your God

whether it be in our consideration of the Father, the Son, or the Holy Spirit, may our response be to acknowledge that these things are 'too wonderful for me'. May these meditations be to the glory of God and the edification of His people and may our devotion to God's service be deepened as we await the Lord's coming.

John Bennett
July 2011

The Holy Trinity
Malcolm Horlock, Cardiff, Wales

(All scripture quotations are from NKJV unless otherwise stated)

'In no other subject is error more dangerous, or inquiry more laborious, or the discovery of truth more profitable', AUGUSTINE, *On the Trinity, Book* 1, Chapter 3, Paragraph 5.

1. What we mean when we speak of the Holy Trinity

The expression 'the Holy Trinity' does not occur in the Bible. But this does not mean that the doctrine is in any way unscriptural; neither do such words as 'substitution', 'sovereignty', 'providence' or 'incarnation'. What matters is whether or not the doctrines conveyed by these words are scriptural. We begin therefore by asking, 'What do we mean when we say that we believe in the Holy Trinity?' We then need to satisfy ourselves that this meaning is in full accord with God's word.

Basically, we mean three things. We believe:
(a) In the unity of the Godhead. That is, that there is one God, and not three.
(b) In the deity of the Father and of the Son and of the Spirit. That is, that each of the Three can be properly described as 'God' in the fullest sense of the word.
(c) That the Father, the Son and the Spirit are personally distinct. That is, that the Father is neither the Son nor the Spirit, and that the Son is not the Spirit.

2. Matthew 28. 19-20

The closing verses of Matthew's Gospel provide a good starting point because the concise statement of verse 19 furnishes us with our Lord's own authority for each of the three statements made in paragraph 1.

When commissioning His disciples, the Lord Jesus spoke both of the authority that was His ('All authority has been given to me') and of the task that was theirs ('Go therefore, and . . .'). Happily for them He links these two statements with the promise that '*I* (the One who has the authority) am with *you* (who have the task)'. The Lord spoke clearly of their duty to baptize all disciples 'in ('into', literally) the name of the Father and of the Son and of the Holy Spirit'. In effect this meant that converts were enlisted into the service of the Triune God. The Jews circumcised their children and proselytes 'in the name of the covenant . . .

9

denoting both entry into the covenant and commitment to it'.[1] That is, by circumcision Jews were brought under the authority and control of the covenant. When Paul wrote of the children of Israel who came out of Egypt that 'all were baptized into Moses in the cloud and in the sea',[2] he was saying that they had identified themselves with Moses and had submitted themselves to his authority and leadership.[3] In a similar way, when baptized in the name of the Triune God, Christian converts identified themselves with, and expressed their allegiance to, the Holy Trinity.

First, we must understand what Jesus meant by, 'the name'. A Hebrew did not regard a name as a mere label or means of identification. A name said something about the person who carried it. To the Jews a person's name expressed what the person was. We might think for instance of the words of Abigail concerning her husband Nabal: 'as his name is, so is he: Nabal (meaning 'folly') is his name, and folly is with him'.[4] For this reason the Old Testament frequently draws attention to the significance of names.[5] A name, then, often signified not so much *who* a person was as *what* he was. The Being of God likewise found expression in His Name. Pre-eminently, in the Old Testament, 'the Name' signified 'Jehovah': 'this glorious and awesome name, the Lord your God'.[6] In the period between the Testaments (when Jews ceased to use the word 'Jehovah', out of a curious mixture of reverence and superstition) 'the Name' became one of the popular substitutes for 'Jehovah'. When in John chapter 17 verse 6, our Lord said, 'I have manifested your name',[7] He meant much the same as that which John had said of Him in chapter 1, 'He has declared Him ('He has made Him known')'.[8]

There is no mistaking the implication of His words in Matthew chapter 28 verse 19, 'baptizing them in the name of the Father and of the Son and of the Holy Spirit'. We should note the exact words He used.

---

[1] *Theological Dictionary of the New Testament* (abridged in one volume), pgs. 697-698.
[2] 1 Cor. 10. 2.
[3] 'He turned the sea into dry land; they went through the river on foot', Ps. 66. 6. 'The children of Israel are the only people of whom I know who were properly baptized without even getting their feet wet!' (My comments on 1 Corinthians 10. 1-4 in *Precious Seed*. Volume 61, Number 3, August 2006.)
[4] 1 Sam. 25. 25.
[5] See, for example, Gen. 3. 20 (Eve means 'living'); 4. 1 (Cain means 'gotten'); 5. 29 (Noah means 'rest' or 'comfort'), 17. 17-19 (Isaac means 'laughter').
[6] Deut. 28. 58.
[7] John 17. 6.
[8] John 1. 18.

(a) 'The name'. The Saviour does not say, 'the names of the Father', etc. Nor does He say, 'the name of the Father, the name of the Son', etc. The single Name embraces the three Persons. And by speaking as He does the Lord Jesus emphasizes the divine unity. There are not three separate Beings.[9]

(b) 'Of the Father and of the Son and of the Holy Spirit'. The Three are united in the single Name. The Three together can be correctly described by the one 'name', which to Jews was the equivalent of 'Jehovah', the only true God.

(c) The repeated article 'the' emphasizes the distinction of the Persons. The Three are not passing phases or modes of one Person. There are three distinct Persons.[10]

These truths are well illustrated by an ancient diagram.

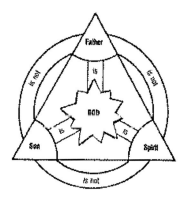

The Lord should be understood therefore as enlarging the name 'Jehovah' into that of 'the Father and of the Son and of the Holy Spirit'. He identified the Lord God of Israel with the Father and the Son and the Holy Spirit, and, in so doing, ascribed a threefold personality to Jehovah.

And so, a Gospel which more or less commences with the record of *a manifestation of the Persons* of the Trinity (at the banks of Jordan, when the Son

---

[9] 'The common name . . . expresses the unity of being', *Theological Dictionary of the New Testament*, Volume V, pg. 274.

[10] We read therefore of the three Persons of the Godhead speaking to one another; e.g. Mark 1. 11; Heb. 1. 8; Matt. 11. 25-26; Rom. 8. 26; and acting towards each other – for example, in sending or being sent, Gal. 4. 4, 6, or in glorifying one another, John 16. 14; 17. 1.

is baptized, the Spirit descends and the Father speaks[11]) closes with *an affirmation of the doctrine* of the Trinity.

3. The New Testament evidence

The New Testament contains no carefully formulated statement of the doctrine of the Holy Trinity such as we find later in the creeds of the established church.[12] Indeed, I know of no reference to the word 'Trinity' until late in the second century, when Theophilus of Antioch used the Greek word '*trias*'. A little later, Tertullian used its Latin equivalent '*trinitas*'. We should not draw wrong conclusions from this. The fact that the New Testament contains no precise definition or systematic treatment of the subject does not mean that the subject had not been carefully thought about in apostolic days. And we possess in its various books more than enough data for us to establish clearly what the early church believed.

To substantiate the truth of the doctrine of the Holy Trinity biblically, we will need to firmly establish each of the three propositions in paragraph 1 above; namely, (a) that there is one God, (b) that the Father, Son and Spirit are each properly described as God, and (c) that the Father, Son and Spirit are each personally distinct from one another.

A. There is one God

This is the fundamental article of faith of both the Jewish nation and the Old Testament, 'Hear, O Israel, Jehovah our God is one Jehovah', Deut. 6. 4 JND.[13] These words have been repeated twice every day for many centuries as part of the Jewish liturgy. The ideal attitude for a Jew was represented in the conduct of Rabbi Akiba of the first century, who, in the hour of his execution, continued to repeat the single word 'One'. The Lord Himself reiterated the words of Deuteronomy chapter 6 verse 4 when He summarized the law, 'The first of all

---

[11] Matt. 3. 16, 17. Compare the mention of the three persons of the Trinity in connection with the coming of the Holy Spirit on the day of Pentecost, Acts 2. 33.

[12] The Athanasian Creed, for example, commences: 'We worship God in Trinity and Trinity in unity, neither confounding the Persons nor dividing the substance. For there is one Person of the Father, another of the Son and another of the Holy Spirit. But the Godhead of the Father, of the Son and of the Holy Spirit is all one, the glory equal and the majesty coequal'.

[13] Literally, 'Jehovah our God Jehovah one'. 'The significance of this paragraph is reflected in the fact that it became the centrepiece of Jewish daily worship, the Keri'at Shema‘ ("Recitation of the Shema"), named for its first word', *The Jewish Publication Torah Commentary*. For the fact that Jehovah alone is God see also Deut. 4. 35, 39.

the commandments is: "Hear, O Israel, the Lord our God, the Lord is one"'.[14]

The unity of the Godhead lay at the foundation of all Paul's teaching. For example, 'there is one God, who will justify the circumcised by faith and the uncircumcised through faith', and 'there is one God, and one mediator'.[15] Nor was Paul alone of course. We note the words of James, 'you believe that there is one God. You do well. Even the demons believe – and tremble'.[16]

That there is one God is a belief therefore that Christians shared with both Jews and demons. The 'fool' says, 'There is no God', Ps. 14. 1. Idolaters say, 'There are many gods', 1 Cor. 8. 6. But Christians say, 'There is one God'!

'Thus says the Lord, the King of Israel, and his Redeemer, the Lord of hosts: "I am the First and I am the Last; besides me there is no God"', Isa. 44. 6.[17] We emphasize that we do not worship three gods; the Father, Son and Spirit are not three separate Beings.

B. The Father, Son and Spirit are each properly described as God

B.1. The Father is God

We do not need to adduce a great deal of evidence for this. It should be sufficient to refer to the many occurrences of the expression 'God the Father'.[18]

B.2. The Son is God

Ever since New Testament days this statement has been attacked and challenged. Yet the evidence is overwhelming. We will briefly examine a sevenfold proof:

(i) *Passages which directly assert the Godhead of the Son.*
(a) Both the commencement and the climax of John's Gospel assert the full deity of our Lord: (i) 'In the beginning was the Word, and the Word was with God, and the Word was God', John 1. 1[19], and (ii) 'Thomas answered and said to Him,

---

[14] Mark 12. 29.
[15] Rom. 3. 30; 1 Tim. 2. 5. See also 1 Cor. 8. 4; Gal. 3. 20.
[16] Jas. 2. 19.
[17] See also Isa. 43. 10; 44. 8; 45. 5, 14, 18, 21, 22; 46. 9; 47. 8; 55. 5.
[18] For example, Gal. 1. 3; Eph. 6. 23; Phil. 2. 11.
[19] Other passages using the Greek word for God (*theos*) without the definite article in a similar construction are always rendered 'God', e.g. Mark 12 .27; Luke 20. 38; John 3. 2; 13. 3; Phil. 2. 13; Heb. 9. 14.

"My Lord and my God!"', John 20. 28[20]. (b) 'Who are Israelites . . . of whom, as according to flesh, is the Christ, who is over all, God blessed for ever', Rom. 9. 5 JND. (c) 'The blessed hope and glorious appearing of our great God and Saviour Jesus Christ', Titus 2. 13.[21] According to Acts chapter 19 verse 27, the Ephesians had a 'great goddess' (Artemis/Diana), but, according to Titus chapter 2 verse 13, the Christian has a 'great God' – Jesus Christ. (d) 'The righteousness of our God and Saviour Jesus Christ', 2 Pet. 1. 1 RV and JND.[22] Thus John, Paul and Peter unite in giving the title 'God' to the Lord Jesus.

(ii) *Passages which indirectly assert the deity of Christ.*[23]
For example:
(a) *His eternal existence.* 'I say to you, before Abraham was, I AM'.[24] For the Saviour to have said, 'before Abraham, I was' would have been no more than a claim to an existence prior to Abraham – a claim such as Michael the archangel could have made. Instead, Jesus asserted His self-existence and eternal being; that He was none less than the great 'I AM' of Exodus chapter 3 verse 14.[25]
(b) *His immutability.* 'Jesus Christ is the same yesterday, today, and forever', Heb. 13. 8.
(c) *His omniscience.* '*If* the mighty works which were done in you had been done

---

[20] Compare Rev. 4. 11, where the same construction is used in the plural ('our') instead of the singular ('my').

[21] The King James Version 'fails to bring out the deity of the Lord Jesus expressed very clearly in the Greek text. The latter conforms to the rule of Greek syntax known as Granville Sharp's rule, which states that when two nouns are in the same case and connected by *kai*, the first noun, articular, the second, anarthrous, the latter always relates to the same person or thing expressed or described by the first noun and is a farther description of it', Dana and Mantey, *A Manual Grammar of the Greek New Testament*, page 147. For the title 'great God' in the Old Testament, see Deut. 10. 17; Ezra 5. 8; Neh 8. 6; Ps. 95. 3; Prov. 26. 10; Dan 2. 45.

[22] Again the King James Version 'fails to bring out the deity of the Lord Jesus expressed very clearly in the Greek text'; see note 21.

[23] The Lord Jesus knew that the acts of power which He had performed in the villages and towns of Galilee would have brought Tyre, Sidon and even Sodom to their knees in repentance. Note that our Lord does not say, '*If* . . . they *might* have', but '*If* . . . they/it *would* have'.

[24] John 8. 58. This is one of three instances where the Lord Jesus asserted His deity in discussion with the Jews; John 5. 18-19; 8. 58-59 and 10. 30-39. In each instance, the Jews understood His claim to be that of equality with God and therefore attempted to kill Him, stone Him and arrest Him, respectively.

[25] 'He does not contrast Abraham's previous existence with His eternity of existence, but Abraham's coming into existence with His eternal being. There is a contrast between Abraham as a created being and our Lord as uncreated, the self-existent, eternal God'. KENNETH S. WUEST, *Bibliotheca Sacra*, July 1962, pg. 221.

in Tyre and Sidon, they *would* (not, we note, '*might*') have repented long ago in sackcloth and ashes'.[26] Only God can know for sure that 'if' such an event happened then certain consequences would follow.[27] Only God knows how every man, woman and child *would have* acted *if* their circumstances had been different to what they were. We mere mortals can only speculate.

(d) *His omnipotence.* His 'name shall be called Wonderful Counselor, *Mighty God*', Isa. 9. 6 ESV.[28] The use of the title 'Mighty God' should be compared in its use in the following chapter, 'The remnant will return, the remnant of Jacob, to the *Mighty God* (which clearly refers to the Lord God)'.[29]

Note separately that those who, when speaking to Peter, Jesus described as 'my sheep' ('Shepherd {the Greek verb ποιμαινω} my sheep', John 21. 16 JND), Peter later describes as 'the flock of God' ('Shepherd {ποιμαινω} the flock of God', 1 Pet. 5. 2 JND.

(iii) *Passages which ascribe Old Testament divine titles to the Lord Jesus.*

(a) *Jehovah.* (i) 'In the name of Jesus every knee should bow, of things in heaven and things on earth and things under the earth, and that every tongue should confess that Jesus Christ is Lord', Phil. 2. 10 RV; compare, 'I the Lord . . . I am God, and there is none else. By myself have I sworn, the word is gone forth from my mouth in righteousness, and shall not return, that unto me every knee shall bow, every tongue shall swear', Isa. 45. 21-23 RV. (ii) 'All the churches shall know that I am He who searches the minds and hearts', Rev. 2. 23; compare, 'I the Lord search the mind and try the heart', Jer. 17. 10 RSV. (iii) Compare also; Matt. 3. 3 with Isa. 40. 3; Rom. 10. 13 with Joel 2. 32; Eph. 4. 8 with Ps. 68. 18; Heb.1. 6 with Ps. 97. 7; 1 Pet. 2. 3-4 with Ps. 34. 8.[30] The confession 'Jesus is Lord' was the central confession of the early church, Rom. 10. 9; 1 Cor. 12. 3.

(b) *God (Elohim).* 'To the Son He says: Your throne, O God, is forever and ever; a sceptre of righteousness is the sceptre of your kingdom', Heb.1. 8-9; compare 'Your throne, O God, is forever and ever; a sceptre of righteousness is the sceptre of your kingdom', Ps. 45. 6-7.

---

[26] Matt. 11. 21; cf. v. 23.
[27] Compare Jer. 38.17-18; and especially 1 Sam. 23. 12-13.
[28] 'Father of eternity' may well mean simply eternal; compare other names formed with word 'father': *Abi-albon*, 'father of strength' = strong (2 Sam. 23. 31); *Abiasaph*, 'father of gathering' = gatherer (Exod. 6. 24); *Abigail*, a woman's name(!), 'father of joy/exultation' = exulting (1 Sam. 25. 3 and 1 Chr. 2. 16).
[29] Isa. 10. 21. See too Jer. 32. 18.
[30] The repeated 'for' in this passage identifies the 'Lord' of Romans chapter 10 verses 12-13 as the 'Lord Jesus' of verse 9.

(c) *The Lord of hosts*. (i) 'Sanctify in your hearts Christ as Lord', 1 Pet. 3. 15 RV; compare, 'The Lord of hosts, Him shall ye sanctify; and let Him be your fear', Isa. 8. 13 RV. (ii) 'The stone which the builders rejected (the Lord Jesus), the same was made the head of the corner; and a stone of stumbling, and a rock of offence', 1 Pet. 2. 7-8 RV; compare, 'He (the Lord of hosts) will be a stone of stumbling and a rock of offence to both the houses of Israel', Isa. 8. 14. (iii) Compare also: John 12. 38-41 with Isa. 6. 3, 10; and note that John 12. 37 clearly identifies the 'Him' of verse 41 as the Lord Jesus.

(d) *The First and the Last*. 'He laid His right hand on me, saying, "Do not be afraid; I am the First and the Last. I am He who lives, and was dead, and behold, I am alive forevermore"', Rev. 1. 17; compare, 'Thus says the Lord, the King of Israel, and his Redeemer, the Lord of hosts: "I am the First and I am the Last; besides me there is no God"', Isa. 44. 6. It is worth noting that the Lord God is called 'the First and the Last' three times in the Old Testament – always in Isaiah, Isa. 41. 4; 44. 6; 48. 12, and that the Lord Jesus is called 'the First and the Last' three times in the New Testament – always in the book of the Revelation, Rev. 1. 17; 2. 8; 22. 13.

(e) *The Ancient of Days*. 'The Ancient of Days was seated . . . the hair of His head was like pure wool', Dan. 7. 9; compare, 'One like the Son of Man . . . His head and hair were white like wool', Rev. 1. 13-14.

(f) *'The Same'* ('The existing One who does not change'[31]). 'To the Son He (God) says . . . You, Lord, in the beginning laid the foundation of the earth . . . they will be changed. But you are *the same*', Heb. 1. 10-12; compare, 'Of old you laid the foundation of the earth, and the heavens are the work of your hands. They will perish, but you will endure; yes, they will all grow old like a garment; like a cloak you will change them, and they will be changed. But you are *the same*, and your years will have no end', Ps. 102. 25-27.

(g) *'The Rock'*. 'They drank of that spiritual Rock that followed them, and that Rock was Christ', 1 Cor. 10. 4[32]; compare, 'Ascribe greatness to our God. He is

---

[31] See the footnotes in JND's New Translation to Deut. 32. 39 and Heb. 1. 12.

[32] In his statement that 'Christ' was the 'spiritual Rock that followed them', 1 Cor. 10. 4, Paul was giving the word 'rock' a double meaning. The apostle has in mind the fact that the water which God gave Israel to drink had (on at least two occasions) come quite literally from a rock, Exod. 17. 1-7; Num. 20. 1-13. But, by playing on the word, he switches the meaning *from* a literal rock *to* a well-known title of God Himself – '*the* Rock'. It is worth noting that this particular title of God occurs five times in Deuteronomy chapter 32. It was Christ, Paul is saying, who accompanied Israel through the wilderness –

the Rock', Deut. 32. 4.[33]

Although not a direct reference to the Old Testament, it is useful also to note the title 'King of kings and Lord of lords', which is ascribed to God in 1 Timothy chapter 6 verses 15-16, and to the Lord Jesus in Revelation chapter 19 verse 16 (cf. Rev. 19. 14).

(iv) *Passages which speak of the Lord Jesus being worshipped.* For example, Matt. 28. 9, 17 (where He did not reject worship the worship of either the women or the eleven disciples). Note also that 'when He again brings the firstborn into the world, He says, Let all the angels of God worship Him', Heb. 1. 6, when is the more pointed when read in the light of the angel's replies to John in both Revelation chapter 19 verse 10 and Revelation chapter 22 verse 8, 'I fell at his feet to worship him. But he said to me, 'See that you do not do that! I am your fellow servant . . . Worship God!' It is interesting to note the limited use of the word 'worship' in Luke's Gospel, which occurs only in Luke chapter 4 verses 7-8 and Luke chapter 24 verse 52. It is, as our Lord said, the Father's purpose that 'all should honour the Son just as they honour the Father', John 5. 23.[34]

(v) *Passages which record thanksgiving and prayer addressed to the Lord Jesus.* First, the example of Stephen; 'they stoned Stephen, praying, and saying, Lord Jesus, receive my spirit. And kneeling down, he cried with a loud voice, Lord, lay not this sin to their charge', Acts 7. 59, 60.[35] Second, the example of Paul; (i) 'there was given to me a thorn in the flesh, a messenger of Satan to buffet me, that I should not be exalted overmuch. Concerning this thing I besought the Lord thrice, that it might depart from me. And he hath said unto me, My grace is sufficient for thee: for my power is made perfect in weakness. Most gladly therefore will I rather glory in my weaknesses, that the power of Christ may rest upon me', 2 Cor. 12. 7-9 RV,[36] and 'I thank Christ Jesus our Lord who has enabled me, because He counted me faithful, putting me into the ministry, although I was formerly a blasphemer, a persecutor, and an insolent man', 1 Tim. 1. 12-13.

---

and it was therefore 'Christ' who they 'tempted' there, 1 Cor. 10. 9. It was, Paul is saying, Christ who constantly provided them with water to drink, and who therefore was their true source of refreshment for forty years.

[33] See also Deut. 32. 5, 18, 30, 31; cf. Ps. 62. 2, 6.

[34] See note 24 above.

[35] Note how Stephen's prayers echo our Lord's own prayers in Luke chapter 23 verses 34 and 46.

[36] Note that 'the Lord' to whom Paul prayed must have been the Lord Jesus because His 'my power' is spoken of by Paul as 'the power of Christ'.

(vi) *Passages where doxologies are ascribed to Him.* Peter and Paul both close their last extant letters with very similar expressions concerning the Lord Jesus; 'to Him be glory forever and ever', 2 Tim. 4. 18; 'to Him be the glory both now and forever', 2 Pet. 3. 18. John, similarly, says concerning the Lord Jesus, 'to Him be glory and dominion forever and ever', Rev. 1. 5, 6.

(vii) *Passages which ascribe divine functions to the Lord.* I do not point to His miracles because any man can perform miracles with divinely communicated power.[37] I refer rather to those works and prerogatives which belong exclusively to God, such as (a) creation, John 1. 3; Col. 1. 16; Heb. 1. 10; (b) providence and preservation, Col. 1. 17; Heb. 1. 3; (c) knowing the hearts of men, John 2. 25 (with 1 Kgs 8. 39[38]; 2 Chr. 6. 30), (d) the forgiving of sins, Mark 2. 5-12[39], and (e) the final raising of the dead and the settling of men's eternal destinies, John 5. 21-27.

B.3. The Spirit is God[40]

In Acts chapter 5, Peter implied clearly that to lie to the Holy Spirit was to lie to God, 'Peter said, "Ananias, why has Satan filled your heart to lie to the Holy Spirit . . . You have not lied to men but to God"'.[41] Equally clearly, Paul implied that to be a temple of the Holy Spirit was one and the same as to be the temple of God.[42] And John implied that to be born of the Spirit, John 3. 6, was to be born of God, 1 John 5. 4.[43]

Only God can know God in His fullness, yet 'the Spirit searches all things, yes, the deep things of God'.[44] There is nothing, not even in God, which baffles His scrutiny.[45] And the Holy Spirit is not only omniscient, but omnipresent; 'Where', David asked, 'can I go from your Spirit?'[46] The Holy Spirit is also eternal; 'Christ, who through the eternal Spirit offered Himself without spot to God'.[47]

---

[37] See also 2 Thess. 2. 9.
[38] Solomon prayed, 'You alone know the hearts of all the sons of men'.
[39] Ultimately only God can forgive sins, for ultimately all sins are committed against God.
[40] See further, *'The Person of the Holy Spirit: Part 1'*, JOHN F. WALVOORD, *Bibliotheca Sacra*, April 1940, pgs. 166-189.
[41] Acts 5. 3, 4.
[42] 1 Cor. 6. 19; 2 Cor. 6. 16.
[43] See also 2 Cor. 3. 17, 18 ('the Lord the Spirit').
[44] 1 Cor. 2. 10.
[45] 1 Cor. 2. 10, 11.
[46] Ps. 139. 7.
[47] Heb. 9. 14.

C. The Father, Son and Holy Spirit are each personally distinct from one another

It is important to have clear in our minds the distinction between the Persons of the Holy Trinity. There is little difficulty in proving the distinction between the Father and the Son. We read frequently of the Father having sent the Son.[48] We also read that the Father addressed the Son,[49] and that the Son addressed the Father in prayer.[50]

However, we need to ask a question about the Holy Spirit which it is unnecessary to ask about either the Father or the Son; namely, 'Is it correct to speak of the Spirit as a Person?'

We answer an emphatic 'Yes' for the following reasons.

(i) *The way in which scripture speaks of the Holy Spirit.* Jesus claimed that the Father would give 'another Helper (or 'Counsellor')' to His disciples,[51] where the word translated 'another' (*allos*) suggests 'another of the same kind'.[52] That is, the Holy Spirit is as much a Person as is the Lord Jesus. Again, the Holy Spirit is often referred to by the Greek masculine pronoun not the neuter pronoun.[53]

(ii) *The actions which are ascribed to Him.* He speaks (e.g. Acts 1. 16; 8. 29), referring to Himself as 'I', Acts 10. 19, 20; He warns, Acts 20. 23; He forbids, Acts 16. 6; He appoints, Acts 20. 28; He sends, Acts 13. 4; He bears witness, John 15. 26; He prevents, Acts 16. 7; He predicts, 1 Pet. 1. 11; He groans, Rom. 8. 26; He leads, Luke 4. 1; Rom. 8. 14; He intercedes, Rom. 8. 27; He loves, Rom. 15. 3; He wills, 1 Cor. 12. 11; He helps, Acts 2. 4; Rom. 8. 26; He encourages, Acts 9. 31; He knows, 1 Cor. 2. 11; He shows, Heb. 9. 8; He searches, 1 Cor. 2. 10; He guides, John 16. 13; He invites, Rev. 22. 17; He reveals, Luke 2. 26; He teaches, John 14. 26; 1 Cor. 2. 13; He dwells, John 14. 17; 1 Cor. 3. 16; Eph. 2. 22, He gives, Acts 2. 4, etc. The Holy Spirit can be

---

[48] See, for example, 1 John 4. 14.
[49] See Mark 1. 11; John 12. 28; Heb. 1. 8.
[50] See Matt. 11. 25-26; 26. 39, 42; John 17. 1.
[51] John 14. 16.
[52] '*Allos* expresses a numerical difference and denotes "another of the same sort"; *heteros* expresses a qualitative difference and denotes "another of a different sort". Christ promised to send "another Comforter" (*allos*, "another like Himself", not *heteros*), John 14. 16', W. E. VINE, *Expository Dictionary of New Testament Words*, article 'Another'.
[53] For example, 'when He, the Spirit of truth, has come, He will guide you into all truth', 16. 13; cf. John 14. 26; 15. 13; 16. 7-8. The word 'Spirit' in Greek is neuter and grammatical considerations sometimes require a neuter pronoun; e.g., John 14. 16-18.

grieved, lsa. 63. 10; Eph. 4. 30; He can be *tempted,* Acts 5. 9; He can be *resisted,* Acts 7. 51, and He can be *lied to,* Acts 5. 3.

And I note that sometimes the Holy Spirit is closely associated in an action with believers, who are unquestionably persons! For example, we have the words of James, 'it seemed good to the Holy Spirit, and to us',[54] and of the Lord Jesus, 'the Spirit of truth, who proceeds from the Father, He will bear witness about me. And you also will bear witness'.[55] And we have the words of John, 'The Spirit and the Bride say, Come!'[56]

And it would surely be absurd to baptize in the Name of a personal Father and a personal Son and an impersonal influence or energy![57]

4. New Testament references to the Holy Trinity

We find references and allusions to the Holy Trinity throughout the New Testament. We find, for example:

(a) *A salutation.* 'From Him who is . . . from the seven Spirits . . . and from Jesus Christ'.[58]
(b) *A greeting.* 'The foreknowledge of God the Father . . . sanctification of the Spirit . . . the blood of Jesus Christ'.[59]
(c) *A thanksgiving.* 'God chose you . . . through sanctification by the Spirit . . . that you may obtain the glory of our Lord Jesus Christ'.[60]
(d) *A prayer.* 'The Father . . . His Spirit . . . that Christ may dwell'.[61]
(e) *A practical exhortation.* 'Praying in the Holy Spirit . . . the love of God . . . the mercy of our Lord Jesus Christ'.[62]
(f) *A doxology.* 'The grace of our Lord Jesus Christ . . . the love of God . . . the communion of the Holy Spirit'.[63]

---

[54] Acts 15. 28.
[55] John 15. 26, 27 ESV.
[56] Rev. 22. 17.
[57] Matt. 28. 19. Again, references, such as Luke 4. 14; Rom. 15. 13, 19; Gal. 2. 29, provide evidence that 'the Spirit' is personal and is not to be confused with an impersonal 'power'. Else in each case we would be reading of 'the power of the power'!
[58] Rev. 1. 4, 5.
[59] 1 Pet. 1. 2.
[60] 2 Thess. 2. 13-14 ESV.
[61] Eph. 3. 14-17.
[62] Jude 20, 21.
[63] 2 Cor. 13. 14.

Many doctrinal statements also bring together the three Persons of the Trinity:

(g) *Salvation announced.* 'The Lord . . . God also . . . gifts of the Holy Spirit'.[64]
(h) *Salvation experienced.* 'The love of God . . . the renewal of the Holy Spirit . . . through Jesus Christ'.[65]
(i) *Salvation enjoyed.* 'Love of God . . . by the Holy Spirit . . . Christ died'.[66]
(j) *Access.* 'Through Him (Christ) . . . by one Spirit . . . to the Father'.[67]
(k) *Apostasy.* 'Partakers of the Holy Spirit . . . the good word of God . . . the Son of God'.[68]
(l) *Unity.* 'One Spirit . . . one Lord . . . one God and Father'.[69]
(m) *Spiritual Gifts.* 'The same Spirit . . . the same Lord . . . the same God'.[70]

Again, we find whole sections of scripture with a 'Trinitarian' structure:

(n) *Romans 1-8.* In very simple terms, the first eight chapters of Romans can be said to deal with (i) the wrath of God, 1. 3-3. 20; (ii) the work of Christ, 3. 21-7. 24, and (iii) the witness of the Spirit and life in the Spirit, 8. 1-39.
(o) *Ephesians 1. 3-14.* This passage is divided into three by the expression 'the praise of the glory of His grace', v. 6, and 'the praise of His glory', vv. 12, 14. Here we read of election and acceptance by *the Father* in verses 3-6, of redemption and forgiveness through *Christ* in verses 7-12, and of a seal and earnest in *the Spirit* in verses 13-14.[71]
(p) *Hebrews 1 3.* In chapter 1, *God* speaks, vv. 2, 5-8, 10, 13; in chapter 2, *the Son* speaks, vv. 12-13; in chapter 3, *the Spirit* speaks, v. 7
(q) *Hebrews 10. 5-18.* Verses 5-10 speak of the will of the Father; verses 11-14 speak of the work of the Son, and verses 15-18 speak of the witness of the Holy Spirit.

From the above references and passages, we should note:
(i) The wide variety of New Testament authors who contribute these.
(ii) The unstudied and natural way in which the threefold pattern is introduced in

---

[64] Heb. 2. 3, 4.
[65] Tit. 3. 4-6.
[66] Rom. 5. 5-6.
[67] Eph. 2. 18. See also the reference to the three Persons of the Holy Trinity at the close of Ephesians 2. Verses 20 to 22 speak of the Lord Jesus as 'the chief corner stone' of the church, which itself constitutes 'a dwelling place for God in the Spirit'.
[68] Heb. 6. 4-6.
[69] Eph. 4. 4-6.
[70] 1 Cor. 12. 4-6.
[71] We might say that this section teaches that salvation was planned by the Father, was executed by the Son and is applied by the Holy Spirit.

21

each case.

(iii) The varying order in which the three Persons are mentioned. The apostolic writers clearly did not feel compelled to follow the order 'Father, Son, and Holy Spirit'. Indeed, the references and passages cited provide examples of every possible combination. To these writers the order clearly wasn't significant.

Consider *the many things separately attributed to each of the Persons of the Trinity*:

	The Father	The Son	The Holy Spirit
Is eternal	Ps. 90. 2	Mic. 5. 2	Heb. 9. 14
Is holy	John 17. 11	Luke 4. 34; Acts 3. 14	Matt. 1. 18, 20; 3. 11 etc.
Is true/truth	John 7. 28	Rev. 3. 7	1 John 5. 6
Creates	Gen. 1. 1	John 1. 3; Col. 1. 16	Job 33. 4
Searches	Jer. 17. 10	Rev. 2. 23	1 Cor. 2. 10
Raises the dead	Acts 26. 8; 1 Cor. 6. 14	John 5. 28-29	Rom. 8. 11; 1 Pet. 3.18
Is glorious	Eph. 1. 17	1 Cor. 2. 8	1 Pet. 4. 14
Loves	John 16. 27	Eph. 3. 19	Rom. 15. 30
Wills	1 Tim. 2. 4	John 17. 24	1 Cor. 12.11
Invites	Isa. 1. 18 (Come and reason)	Matt. 11. 28 (Come and rest)	Rev. 22. 17 (Come and refresh)
Gives life	1 Tim. 6. 13	John 5. 21	2 Cor. 3. 6
Justifies	Rom. 8. 33	Gal. 2. 17	1 Cor. 6.11
Sanctifies	Jude 1 ('by')	1 Cor. 1. 2 ('in')	1 Pet. 1. 2 ('of')
Indwells	2 Cor. 6. 16	Eph. 3. 17	John 14. 17
Pours out	Tit. 3. 6	Matt. 26. 28	Rom. 5. 5
Known by Christians	1 John 2. 13	1 John 2. 3	1 John 4. 6
Our source of joy	Rom. 5. 11	Phil. 4. 4	1 Thess. 1. 6
Our fellowship with	1 John 1. 3	1 Cor. 1. 9	2 Cor. 13. 14

It is therefore no exaggeration to say that the New Testament is permeated by Trinitarian teaching.

5. The Old Testament

It is obvious to even the most casual reader that the Old Testament offers no developed doctrine of the Holy Trinity.[72] We can, however, say two things at least.

(a) At no time is the teaching of the Old Testament inconsistent with the later revelation given in the New Testament. I note, for instance, that, when the Law says that 'Jehovah our God is one Jehovah' (or possibly, 'Jehovah our God, Jehovah is one'),[73] the Hebrew word translated 'one' can (and often does) include the idea of plurality in unity.[74] The idea conveyed by the word *can*, therefore, be that of 'one made up of more than one'.[75]

(b) There are several clear anticipations of the doctrine.[76] There are, for example, indications of the deity both of the Messiah[77] and of the Holy Spirit.[78] There are also the passages in Genesis and Isaiah where God speaks in terms of 'us': (i) 'Then God said, Let *us* make man in our image, after our likeness'[79]; (ii) 'The Lord God said, "Behold, the man has become like one of *us*, to know good and evil"'[80]; (iii) 'The Lord said . . . Come, let *us* go down and there confuse their language'[81]; and (iv) 'I heard the voice of the Lord saying, "Whom shall I send, and who will go for *us*?"'[82]

---

[72] Personally I would not appeal to the plural '*elohim*' as evidence for plurality within the Godhead. I note, for example, that the plural '*elohim*' is used to describe Ba'al, Judg. 6. 31, Dagon, Judg. 16. 23-14, and even Samuel, 1 Sam. 28. 13.

[73] Deut. 6. 4.

[74] See, for example, Gen. 2. 24; Num. 13. 23; Judg. 21. 6; Ezek. 37. 17.

[75] See *New International Dictionary of Old Testament Theology and Exegesis*, Volume 4, pages 1217-1218. I am certainly not claiming that Deuteronomy chapter 6 verse 4 teaches the doctrine of the Trinity. But I think it fair to say that the verse is wholly consistent with it.

[76] See the reference to all three Persons of the Trinity in Isaiah chapter 42 verse 1 and possibly in Isaiah chapter 48 verse 16.

[77] Isa. 9. 6; Zech. 13. 7; Mic. 5. 2.

[78] 2 Sam. 2. 2-3; Job 26. 13; Pss. 104. 30; 139. 7.

[79] Gen. 1. 26. Clearly 'our image' is one and the same as 'the image of God', v. 27. That God was not talking to angels is clear therefore because, referring to the creation of man, the writer declares, 'in the image of God created He him'. God never created man in the image of angels, but in the divine image alone.

[80] Gen. 3. 22.

[81] Gen. 11. 6-7.

[82] Isa. 6. 8.

Behold your God

We may wonder why it was that the full revelation of the truth about the Triune God was held back until New Testament times. We are not told but two observations may help us:

(i) I suspect that an early revelation of the Triune God might have proved dangerous. As it was, Israel showed a constant tendency to idolatry and polytheism. It was wise therefore that the fact that there is only one God should be fixed firmly in their minds before the fuller revelation of one God in three Persons was given.

(ii) It was far easier for men to grasp and to accept the doctrine of the Trinity after the incarnation of the Son and after the coming of the Holy Spirit at Pentecost.[83]

6. Understanding and faith

Not that it is possible for any human mind to grasp how three Persons can exist in one Being. We believe the doctrine of the Trinity, not because we understand it, but because the Bible teaches it. We are altogether unable to fathom the depths of the divine Being, and the doctrine of the Holy Trinity must therefore remain a sublime mystery which transcends human thought.[84] But God has spoken, and it is enough!

7. The different roles and functions of the Persons of the Holy Trinity

In the outworking of their eternal purpose and their counsels for time, the Persons of the Godhead have adopted different roles and perform different functions.[85]

This must not be understood in terms of human arrangements, such as superiority-inferiority. But, although ever remaining equal with Him in nature

---

[83] Indeed, the early Christians' very real Trinitarian experience necessitated a doctrinal explanation. For that experience, see, for example, 'through Him (the Lord Jesus) we both have access by one Spirit to the Father', Eph. 2. 18.

[84] It has been said of the doctrine of the Trinity: 'Set out to understand it, and you'll lose your mind. But set out to deny it, and you'll lose your soul!'

[85] See the Additional Note to John 14. 28 in B. F. WESTCOTT's 'Commentary on the Gospel of John'. Consider the statement, 'Her Majesty Queen Elizabeth II is greater than I'. Clearly, I mean that she is greater than I am in terms of wealth, authority, status, influence, renown etc. No-one would take me to mean that she is more of a human being than I am.
See further: https://www.cbmw.org/images/jbmw_pdf/15_2/10.pdf.

and being, the Son and Spirit act in subjection to the Father. The Father sent the Son into the world,[86] and the Father and the Son sent the Spirit.[87] Throughout, the Father, the Son and the Holy Spirit co-operate in the administration of that eternal purpose which knows neither defeat nor frustration, and which will be consummated when 'God' is 'all in all'.[88]

It should surely fill us all with wonder and amazement that we should be the objects of the eternal purpose of the Triune God.

'The grace of the Lord Jesus Christ, and the love of God, and the communion of the Holy Spirit be with you all'.

---

[86] Gal. 4. 4; 1 John 4 14.
[87] John 14. 26; 15. 26; 16. 7.
[88] 1 Cor. 15. 28.

The Power of God
Andrew Mellish, Vancouver, Canada

If we were to talk to one of our neighbours, or take a random survey in the local High Street, and ask for some descriptive words about God, I think it would be safe to say that the word 'power', or 'powerful', would be placed on the list very quickly. Further, whenever men have made up their own ideas of gods, in some capacity they will attribute some level of power to their god. There is something within all men that wants to attribute power to God, and, even in the case of the pagan, his gods.

When we come to the scriptures, we are faced not with a God who says He is powerful, but, by His actions, He demonstrates His power, and it is primarily this aspect that we will focus on in this chapter. Before doing so, it will be worthwhile to consider the different uses of the word as we come upon them in the scriptures.

Rather remarkably, the exact expression 'power of God' is not found in the Old Testament, and the first person to use this expression was the Lord Himself, Matt. 22. 29, where He accused the Sadducees of not knowing the scriptures, nor the 'power of God'. If we lift this verse off the page of scripture in application for the current purpose, we can take from it that it is only by knowing, or, more accurately, discerning or perceiving the scriptures that we can come to a full appreciation of the power of God.

According to W. E. VINE, the use of the word in scripture describes for us God's ability, might, dominion, strength, and authority. There are two words that highlight God's power as one of His attributes. The first is the Greek word *dynamis*, and this, according to STRONG's Lexicon, is inherent power, power residing in a thing by virtue of its nature, or which a person or thing exerts and puts forth. The psalmist may well ask the question, 'For who in the heaven can be compared unto the Lord? who among the sons of the mighty can be likened unto the Lord?' Ps. 89. 6. For us, as we come to an understanding of scripture, this makes it significantly easier to comprehend that power is clearly a rightful attribute of God.

Another word used in scripture is the word *exousia*, and again we are indebted to W. E. VINE as he shows that it is 'the freedom of action, right to act', and, when used of God, it is absolute, and unrestricted, e.g., 'But I will forewarn you whom ye shall fear: Fear him, which after he hath killed hath power to cast into hell; yea, I say unto you, Fear him', Luke 12. 5. Yet, in every generation men in their ignorance rail against God with, they think, impunity!

The use of the word 'power' is also applied to Christ and His miracles; men, and authority that is delegated to them; and angels who, in Ephesians chapter 3 verse 10, are described as 'powers'.

Display of God's Power

Anyone looking for a description of God and opening a Bible at the first chapter and verse would be in awe as they see a demonstration of His power as the creation of this world is brought before them. In this demonstration of power we begin to learn about the character of God, as we see, for example, order and variety, and a remarkable expression of power as He creates the worlds out of nothing. As we see the order that God brings to the days of creation, we also begin to appreciate something of the mind of God. Job would have appreciated this when, in chapter 38, God speaks to him, and, in a series of questions, begins to show Job that His power had order to it, it was a power that did not introduce things randomly, 'Where wast thou when I laid the foundations of the earth? declare, if thou hast understanding. Who hath laid the measures thereof, if thou knowest? or who hath stretched the line upon it? Whereupon are the foundations thereof fastened? or who laid the corner stone thereof?' Job 38. 4-6. God, completely, and independently!

Outside of the creation of Adam, when we think of the physical creation of the world, there are two expressions that sum up God's power in the creation. Firstly, 'And God said, Let there be light: and there was light', Gen. 1. 3. 'How simple! And yet how Godlike!' C. H. MACKINTOSH. 'He spake, and it was done. He commanded, and it stood fast', Ps. 33. 9. The unregenerate man might ask all the questions, and yet the newest believer can appreciate, by faith, it was by His power that all things came into being.

Secondly, 'he made the stars also', Gen. 1. 16. With the knowledge that men have acquired, *Encyclopedia Britannica* brings the subject of stars under forty-one different sub-sections. While it should not surprise us that there is not one reference to the power of God, we can appreciate that to our God, it was nothing to put the stars in their place. In all their vastness and variety, they are immense distances away from our earth, and yet visible to the naked eye. We can look up and just wonder in amazement, 'he made the stars also'.

Again, we look to the appreciation of the psalmist to demonstrate to us not only God's power in creation but how He moves about His created universe, and in it we can come to value other facets of God. Momentarily, for example, 'He maketh the clouds his chariot: who walketh upon the wings of the wind', Ps. 104.

3. We know the power and force of wind, in hurricanes, and typhoons, and God reveals to us that He 'walks' on the wind. That which sinful man does not have the ability to harness, God simply walks on, and exhibits His absolute power over His creation.

With the establishment of the creation, God has not just stood idly back. His power is seen daily as He 'upholdeth all things by the word of his power', Heb. 1. 3, and, in every aspect of nature, including human life, we see the preserving power of God, for example, of the land from the oceans, or in the womb of a mother as she carries her unborn child. Similarly, God has placed ordered governments of men, and when men have failed to execute this justly, we see His power in judgement upon them.

Designation of God's Power

When God created this world, He gave it to Adam to look after. The psalmist tells us, 'Thou madest him to have dominion over the works of thy hands', Ps. 8. 6, and, as we know, Adam failed miserably. It was always God's intention that power would be invested in a man to be responsible for the creation, and yet, sadly, every dispensation has proven that sinful man does not have the ability to carry out this mandate. In 2011 what is the earth's condition? Our answer is found in Romans chapter 8 verse 22, 'For we know that the whole creation groaneth and travaileth in pain together until now'. Verse 19 of the same chapter tells us that, 'For the earnest expectation of the creature waiteth for the manifestation of the sons of God'.

Beloved, we should be looking for the rapture, when we will see our blessed Lord, but can you take your mind further to the day when wondering worlds will see that Man of Calvary, and, in Christ, God's power (authority) will be designated to Him, the perfect Man, as He sets up His kingdom, and we, with Him, will rule and reign. For the first time, God's original intention will be displayed through His well-beloved Son, and perfect rule will be carried out.

He must have the pre-eminence, and, without taking anything away from Christ, I would exhort us not to lose sight of the truth, that this designation of God's power will be at our disposal too, as we participate in the rule and reign of Christ. Paul reminds the Corinthians, 'Know ye not that we shall judge angels?' 1 Cor. 6. 3, and that we will judge the world. 'To him that overcometh will I grant to sit with me in my throne, even as I also overcame, and am set down with my Father in his throne', Rev. 3. 21.

The earth was created for the habitation of men, and we, who were created in His likeness and image and as those saved by grace, were saved to enable God to have a bride for His Son. John describes us as 'the bride, the Lamb's wife', Rev. 21. 9, we will share His throne and rule over God's universe with Him in power and authority. As God's power is demonstrated at the beginning of time, in all the majesty of the creation, when we come to the end of the Bible, we begin to get a glimpse of the purpose of it all. Just as God saw that it was 'not good that the man should be alone', Gen. 2. 18, God desired a bride for His Son, and, in a future day, presented to Christ without spot or blemish, we will be seated with Him upon the throne, ruling and reigning into all eternity.

The Sovereignty of God
Richard Collings, Caerphilly, Wales
(All scripture quotations are from NKJV unless otherwise stated)

Introduction

Being unique, incomparable, and ineffable, it is impossible for any created intelligence to have a comprehensive knowledge of God, for He is infinitely exalted above all His creatures. Thousands of years ago Zophar said, 'Can you search out the deep things of God? Can you find out the limits of the Almighty? They are higher than heaven – what can you do? Deeper than Sheol – what can you know? Their measure is longer than the earth and broader than the sea', Job 11. 7.

Yet, although He is unfathomable, God is not unknowable for He has chosen to reveal Himself to us. All that we shall ever know about Him, is the result of His choosing to make Himself known. But it doesn't stop there for God is not only knowable but is approachable. Like Abraham, we can say, 'Indeed now, I who am but dust and ashes have taken it upon myself to speak to the Lord', Gen. 18. 27.

As is true of every divine attribute, God's sovereignty is immeasurable. Even if it were possible to have the tongues of men and angels, we would have to agree with the hymn that 'all are to mean to speak His worth'. Therefore, it is important that we embark on this brief consideration of the sovereignty of God with a great sense of awe, and conscious inadequacy.

A definition

Before attempting to give a limited definition of the sovereignty of God there are two points we need to consider. Firstly, the words 'sovereign' and 'sovereignty' do not occur in the Bible. However, that does not mean that God is not sovereign. From the beginning to the end of the scriptures we see the irrefutable evidences of this glorious truth. Secondly, it may be more accurate to suggest that sovereignty is not an attribute of God, rather it is the direct outcome of all His attributes. We say that God is love because love is an intrinsic element of His essential nature rather than because of something that He does or says. However, God is sovereign because He is almighty, spatially unlimited, ever-existing and measureless in knowledge.

Recognizing the limitations of any definition of divine sovereignty, we can state that, because of all that He is, God will achieve everything His perfect will

31

determines. However, a mistake we need to avoid is to think that because He is sovereign God will act in any way contrary to His nature. For example, God cannot lie, Titus 1. 2. Sovereignty is exclusively His prerogative and He does not require the consent of anyone, or anything, to exercise it. Writing to the saints at Ephesus, Paul says of God that He 'works all things according to the counsel of His will', Eph. 1. 11.

An acknowledgment of the sovereignty of God

One of the clearest tributes to the sovereignty of God came not from the lips of a mighty prophet or a faithful priest, nor was it the overflowing worship of some devoted saint, but it was the confession of a heathen monarch. Nebuchadnezzar, the king of Babylon, declared, 'I, Nebuchadnezzar, blessed the most High and praised and honoured him who lives forever: for His dominion is an everlasting dominion and His kingdom is from generation to generation . . . he does according to His will in the army of heaven and among the inhabitants of the earth. No one can restrain His hand', Dan. 4. 34-35. Daniel describes Nebuchadnezzar as a king of kings and, in comparison with his kingdom, all subsequent world empires will be inferior, yet that Babylonian despot was brought to the point where he acknowledged that there is only one Ruler who is sovereign and he describes Him as being 'the most high'.

God's right to be sovereign

World history is littered with the names of people who have occupied a place of authority or power for which they had no merit, or suitability. By conniving, bribery or brute force, they have elevated themselves above their rightful station and exercised an influence they didn't deserve. However, in thinking about God's sovereignty we are contemplating One who not only has the ability, but has the unquestionable entitlement to be sovereign.

God has the ability to be sovereign because of what He is [89] and, in addition, He has the right because of who He is – He is God. His right to be the supreme Governor derives from no other source than Himself. In Isaiah chapter 46, God gives a self-description, which is in direct contrast to the lifeless and powerless gods of the heathen, 'I am God, and there is no other; I am God, and there is none like me', v. 9. In the previous chapter, God proclaims, 'I am the Lord, and

---

[89] God has the ability to be sovereign because He is eternal (not limited to, or by, time), omnipotent (all powerful), omnipresent (not limited by space), immutable (unchanging) and omniscient (all knowing).

there is no other; There is no God besides me . . . that they may know from the rising of the sun to its setting that there is none besides me. I am the Lord, and there is no other', vv. 5-6.

In addition to His inherent right to be sovereign, there is something that God has done that also gives Him that entitlement – for sovereignty presupposes the fact of creation. Without any other influence, for there was no other, God created the heavens and the earth. Before that there was nothing and nowhere save God and His eternal abode. The universe had not been formed, and creation existed only as a blueprint in the counsels of the Almighty, then God spoke 'and it was done; He commanded, and it stood fast', Ps. 33. 9. Furthermore, God created this vast universe for His own pleasure, hence the twenty-four elders in heaven cry out, 'Thou art worthy, O Lord, to receive glory and honour and power: for thou hast created all things, and for thy pleasure they are and were created', Rev. 4. 11 KJV.

A consequence of God's sovereignty

A direct consequence of God's sovereignty is that no one has the right to challenge what He does. Despite this, sin-corrupted and devil-blinded mortals who live on a planet that is miniscule against the backdrop of the universe, and whose lives are just a vapour, frequently question God in a disparaging manner. Such people would do well to heed those words of Nebuchadnezzar, 'All the inhabitants of the earth are reputed as nothing . . . and none can stay his hand or say to Him, What have you done?' Dan. 4. 35.

However, even we who are Christians have to admit there are many times when we cannot understand what God is doing or what He allows. Why did God permit Herod to kill James with the sword and yet miraculously deliver Peter from the same fate? There are many imponderables in life, so many of our questions will remain unanswered and the challenge for us is to acknowledge that because God is infinitely wise He cannot err, and because He is infinitely righteous He will not do wrong. Happy is that believer who doesn't see life as an unfolding drama of inevitable, predetermined consequences in which they are hapless pawns but who bows in faith and says, 'As for God, His way is perfect', Ps. 18. 30.

Another outcome that should derive from God's sovereignty is the peace we ought to enjoy knowing that He is in control. C. H. SPURGEON said, 'There is no attribute more comforting to His children than that of God's sovereignty'. We live in a chaotic world where the unpredictability of nations, climate conditions, financial institutions and of individual behaviour is reaching unprecedented levels. Despite the best efforts of governments and international organizations, these uncertainties continue on an inexorable downward spiral until the time comes when men's hearts will fail them for fear. How grateful we should be, and how reassuring it is to know, that despite the global disarray nothing takes place outside of the sovereign will of God. He dwells in an eternal tranquillity because nothing can overrun the boundaries that His sovereignty has decreed, and, as the Most High, He 'rules in the kingdom of men', Dan. 4. 17.

Demonstrations of God's sovereignty

One sphere in which God stamped His sovereignty is creation, for He was under no obligation to create; that He chose to do so was purely a sovereign act governed by His own good pleasure. At a point He chose, God spoke and from nothing the heavens and the earth were created! When Solomon built the temple in Jerusalem he used great stones, cedar trees, fir trees, iron and brass too heavy to weigh, 100,000 talents of gold and 1,000,000 talents of silver. He employed 183,300 men and it took him seven years to complete. God needed no materials and employed no one, He just spoke, and in six days the universe was complete.

There is another sphere in which God has displayed His sovereignty, a sphere even more amazing than His first creation; it is in the new creation. In Ephesians chapter 1 we discover that God has brought about our salvation by His own will and His own purpose and His own design and to the praise of His own glory. For these reasons Paul describes each Christian as being 'his workmanship', Eph. 2. 10. To create the universe God just spoke and it cost Him nothing; to bring about the new creation God sent His Son - and it cost Him everything. That this was a demonstration of His sovereignty is clearly emphasized by Peter on the day of Pentecost, 'Him, being delivered by the determinate counsel and foreknowledge of God', Acts 2. 23 KJV.

Conclusion

We have hardly scratched the surface of this vast subject; our consideration at best has been but a sketchy introduction. Despite this inadequacy may we make it our ambition to get to know God better for 'thus says the Lord: "Let not the wise man glory in his wisdom, let not the mighty man glory in his might, nor let the rich man glory in his riches; but let him who glories glory in this, that he understands and knows me"', Jer. 9. 23-24.

The Holiness of God
Eric G. Parmenter, Ynysbwl, Wales

No other book sets out the nature and character of God more realistically than the Bible. In it the transcendent glory, majesty, almighty power, righteousness and holiness that characterize Him are all revealed with great clarity.

The basic truth embedded in the word 'holy' is 'to be set apart, to be separate' – God is altogether separate and apart from all that is neither holy nor pure. God in essence is the 'Holy One'. The meaning of holiness in respect of God is stated by John, 'This is the message which we have heard of him . . . God is light and in him is no darkness at all', 1 John 1. 5.

In His purity, majesty and glory God is absolutely and intrinsically holy. At the outset, the Bible emphasizes God's holiness and, throughout, the subject holds sway – God is holy – this truth is stamped indelibly on the pages of scripture. If the actions of God in the Garden of Eden express His righteousness when He drove out the man, setting the cherubim at its entrance with a flaming sword, Gen. 3. 24, then at Sinai, when the law of God was given, the mountain burning with fire expresses His holiness, at which Moses said, 'I exceedingly fear and quake'. God's holiness was further displayed in the wilderness when Moses, approaching the bush that burned with fire, unconsumed, heard God's voice, 'Put off thy shoes from off thy feet, for the place whereon thou standest is holy ground', Exod. 3. 5, indicating that the manifested presence of God in His holiness made the surrounding area where Moses was holy ground. When the tabernacle was set up, Aaron with his sons were given the privilege to draw near to God. Nadab and Abihu, sons of Aaron, approached God, but with strange fire, both being consumed by fire that came out from the Lord God. On that occasion God acted in His holiness as a consuming fire, Lev. 10. 1-2, a solemn reminder that in our priestly service we ought 'to serve God acceptably with reverence and godly fear: for our God is a consuming fire', Heb. 12. 28-29. The holiness of God is the reason behind the dietary laws given to Israel. On the basis of what God is, Moses commanded the people, 'Ye shall be holy, for I am holy', Lev. 11. 44. The same truth is stated in Leviticus chapter 19 verse 2, 'Ye shall be holy: for I the Lord your God am holy'. Israel's relationship to God resulted in His holiness reaching into every department of life. In the New Testament Peter lifts the truth of God's holiness from the references in Leviticus and applies the same principle to believers of this present day. 'But as he which hath called you is holy, so be ye holy in all manner of conversation (behaviour); Because it is written, 'Be ye holy; for I am holy', 1 Pet. 1. 15-16.

Isaiah saw the Lord sitting upon a throne, high and lifted up, whose train filled the temple; the intrinsic holiness of the throne sitter is seen in smoke, the incense of worship; and before the throne the seraphim, crying one to another, 'Holy, holy, holy is the Lord of hosts'. (The tense gives the sense that this was characteristic of their ministry continually). These burning ones are continuously occupied with the holiness of God, in whose presence they cover their faces. Isaiah responded, 'Woe is me, for I am undone'. Any contemplation we might have of God in the beauty and glory of His holiness will bring us to the same place.

Coming to the New Testament, when God was manifested in flesh, the angel's message to Mary was 'that holy thing that shall be born shall be called the Son of God', Luke 1. 35. In the days of His flesh the Lord Jesus manifested the beauty of divine holiness in His sinless life. The quality of that holiness was now displayed in perfection in the Person of Christ. The absolute holiness of God was recognized in the Lord throughout His sojourn here. Demons said, 'We know thee who thou art, the Holy One of God'. The writer to the Hebrews affirms, 'who is holy, harmless, undefiled, separate from sinners'. What He is now in heaven He was on earth in all the polluting atmosphere of sin in which He lived, moved and had His being. At Golgotha, in those hours of darkness when our Lord was 'made sin for us', there is evidenced the holiness of God. God who is of 'purer eyes than to behold evil and canst not look upon iniquity', Hab. 1. 13, forsook the Man of Calvary who had taken responsibility to be the sin bearer – 'My God, my God, why hast thou forsaken me?' The answer – 'But thou art holy', Ps. 22. 1, 3. The implication of this truth for believers today is be holy in all manner of conduct, holy in thought, word and ways, for 'it is written "I am holy", saith the Lord'.

The Love of God
Bernard Osborne, Cardiff, Wales

The apostle John tells us that 'God is love', 1 John 4. 8, 16. It is what He is essentially and eternally. He loves from everlasting. The statement is true quite independently of our being there to be loved. What then was the object of such love so that it could have been satisfied even without being poured out on mankind? We note the words of the Lord Jesus, 'Thou lovedst me before the foundation of the world', John 17. 24. Love in its essential nature exists in relationship and involves self-communication to another, and so if love and fatherhood belong eternally to God, there must be a distinction of Persons within the Godhead. If we conceive of God as always and essentially living and loving, we must accept the doctrine of an eternal Son and Spirit of God. The relationship between the Father and Son is one of love. Most frequently the Father's love for the Son is brought before us.[90] We also learn of the Son's love for the Father.[91]

In the Old Testament the love of God is seen particularly in His relationship with Israel. The Lord chose Israel because He loved her.[92] It was not evoked by any intrinsic worth or qualities in Israel, but was rooted firmly in the personal character of God Himself. God's love has no cause prior to itself. It is not caused by any attractiveness or merit in its object. It is shown to be deeper than that of the love of a mother for her children, Isa. 49. 15. It is pictured in the paternal relationship and the marriage relationship. Israel is God's 'son'.[93] Hosea also poignantly paints the picture of a marriage relationship, and portrays a love that is willing to suffer.[94]

Writers have drawn attention to two types of love, one of complacence, and the other of benevolence. The love of complacence is drawn forth by the worth and excellency of the object. That of benevolence is a love that gives itself to lift the worthless, unlovely and undeserving into purity and beauty. That is the love, boundless and quenchless, which God has demonstrated to sinners. J. I. PACKER wrote, 'There was nothing whatever in the objects of His love to call it forth, nothing in man to attract or prompt it. Among men love is awakened by something in the beloved, but the love of God is free, spontaneous, unevoked, uncaused. God loves men because He has chosen to love them, and no reason for

---

[90] Mark 1. 11; Matt. 12. 18; John 3. 35; 15. 9; 17. 23, 24, 26; Col. 1. 13 NIV.
[91] John 14. 31.
[92] Deut. 4. 37, 38; 7. 6-8; 10. 15; Isa. 43. 4.
[93] Exod. 4. 22, 23; Jer. 31. 20; Hos. 11. 1; Mal. 1. 6.
[94] This marriage metaphor is found elsewhere, Jer. 2. 1; 31. 32; Isa. 54. 5; 62. 4, 5.

His love can be given save His own sovereign good pleasure'. To this we add the words of J. N. DARBY, 'In sovereign grace He rises above the sin, and loves without a motive save what is in His own nature and part of His glory. Men must have a motive for loving, God has none but in Himself, and "commended His love to us in that while we were yet sinners Christ died for us", the best thing in heaven that could be given for the vilest, most defiled and guilty sinners'.

God's love, then, is seen in the exercise of His goodness towards sinners. As such, it expresses itself in grace and mercy. Grace is the bestowal upon sinners of what they do not deserve; mercy is the withholding from sinners of what they deserve.

God manifests His love in giving. This is the characteristic manifestation of love. The measure of love is how much it gives. God's love is measured by the gift of His only begotten Son, John 3. 16, whom He sent into the world to seek and to save the lost, to bring sinners back to Himself, and in the course of this work to suffer at their hands even to death. In the New Testament the cross of Christ is the crowning proof of the reality and boundlessness of God's love.[95] In so far as God desires the salvation of all,[96] and has provided, in the sacrifice of His Son, for the salvation of all,[97] His love embraces the whole world, v. 16. God's love provides the propitiation which averts His wrath upon us, 1 John 4. 10. The Lord Jesus Christ is the propitiatory offering laid on the altar, exposed to the fire of God's wrath, meeting all the claims of divine justice as a perfect sacrifice for the guilty. On the basis of His sacrifice and death the sinner can say, 'God be merciful, be propitious, to me the sinner'.

---

[95] 1 John 4. 9; John 3. 16; Rom. 5. 8.
[96] 1 Tim. 1. 15; 2. 4; 4. 10.
[97] 1 Tim. 2. 6; 1 John 2. 2; 4. 10.

The Faithfulness of God
Eric G. Parmenter, Ynysbwl, Wales

A perusal of the New Testament Epistles reveals a number of direct references to God's faithfulness. 'God/He is faithful' is a recurring statement. 'Faithful' used of God means He is trustworthy, that He can be relied upon, that complete confidence may be placed in Him, and that we may have confidence in Him in the variety of circumstances of life.[98]

The Faithful God and Fellowship

Paul, writing to the church of God at Corinth, indicates the character of their corporate fellowship and then brings together a cluster of blessings, the last being, 'God is faithful, by whom ye were called unto the fellowship of His Son Jesus Christ our Lord', 1 Cor. 1. 9. This is a wonderful privilege; the faithful God willing to share His Son with us is a truth to thrill the heart. Of course, the enjoyment of this fellowship depends upon the spiritual state of the believer.

The Faithful God and Temptations

'No temptation', says Paul, '[hath] taken you, but such as is common to man', 1 Cor. 10. 13. The Christian's trials are but common trials; others have like burdens and temptations. God is faithful, Satan is a deceiver. Men may be false, but God is faithful. Our strength and security are in Him. He will never disappoint His children.

God is wise as well as faithful, and proportions our burden to our strength. He will not allow us to be tempted above what we are able. He will take care that we are not overcome; He will make a way to escape, either from the trial itself or at least the mischief of it. There is no valley so dark but He can find a way through it, no affliction so grievous but He can prevent or remove it, or enable us to support it, and in the end overrule it to our advantage.

The Faithfulness of God and His Promise

---

[98] For example, the blessing of fellowship with God's Son is connected with God's faithfulness, 1 Cor. 1. 9. God is faithful in our trials, 1 Cor. 10. 13. His word is true, i.e., faithful, 2 Cor. 1. 18. He is faithful to His promises, Heb. 10. 23; 11. 11. In circumstances of suffering according to His will, He is a faithful Creator, 1 Pet. 4. 19. He is faithful in His forgiveness, 1 John 1. 9. These scriptures show God's unfailing faithfulness providing for the needs of His people in every experience of life with unremitting regularity.

Behold your God

The writer to the Hebrews having set forth the value of the work of Christ and the witness of the Holy Spirit as to our forgiveness reminds his readers of God's invitation to enter the holiest with boldness and to draw near in full assurance of faith, Heb. 10. 19, 22. Such privileges they were to hold fast. The motive or reason for this is 'he is faithful that promised', v. 23. God has made great and precious promises to believers, and He is true to His word; there is no fickleness with Him. His faithfulness should inspire and encourage us to enter boldly and draw near to God in the full assurance of being forgiven and accepted on the ground of the finished work of Christ.[99]

The Faithfulness of God and Suffering

The apostle Peter majors on the subject of sufferings in his First Epistle, first in relation to the Lord Jesus, secondly in relation to those who are associated with Him, 'if any one suffers as a Christian', 4. 16. Suffering is the lot of every believer. The apostle links the truth of suffering with the 'will of God' and with God as a 'faithful Creator', v. 19. The will of God is introduced to assure us that such sufferings are permitted and controlled by Him having the best in view for us. In the experience of suffering in well-doing we are to commit our souls unto Him who is a faithful Creator. The solitary reference here to God as Creator in the New Testament tells us that He who created us will be faithful in His care of saints.[100]

The Faithfulness of God and Forgiveness

The epistle to the Romans sets out the judicial side of forgiveness of sins. On the basis of the sacrifice of Christ, God has forgiven past, present, and future sins judicially, where faith has been placed in the Lord Jesus Christ. John, in his First Epistle, introduces the subject of God's family. All God's children can live in the enjoyment of fellowship with God and with His Son. That fellowship is disturbed when any of God's children commits a sin. As a result of the advocacy of Christ, the one who has sinned is made conscious of the sin committed. Upon confession of that sin, God is faithful and just to forgive and cleanse from all unrighteousness, 1 John 1. 9. God is liberal in forgiveness because of the

---

[99] Sarah bore a son when she was past age because she reckoned God was faithful who had promised, Heb. 11. 11. She had no other confidence or expectation than the faithfulness of God whose promises are never broken even though a passage of time may elapse. Because God is faithful Sarah believed that what God promised He was able to perform.

[100] This is seen in the first assembly prayer meeting recorded in Acts chapter 4 verses 23-24.

40

provision made in the blood of Christ. Where true confession is made, a faithful God forgives what we did and cleanses from the unrighteousness which issues from the sin committed. Let us then reckon on God's faithfulness to us, 1 Thess. 5. 24.

God who is Longsuffering
Ken Totton, Cambridge, England
(All scripture quotations are from NKJV unless otherwise stated)

We live in an increasingly impatient age. People's 'fuses seem short' and new terms such as 'road-rage' have been coined to denote aggressive behaviour on the highway. Selfish intolerance fuels conflicts and injuries throughout society.

What a refreshing contrast we find in the ways of the eternal God! Throughout the scriptures we delight to read statements such as, 'The Lord is merciful and gracious, slow to anger, and abounding in mercy'.[101]

Proverbs extols this quality, 'He who is slow to anger is better than the mighty, and he who rules his spirit than he who takes a city', Prov. 16. 32. This restraint is seen to perfection in God. He is unhurried, for His timescales are radically different from ours, 'with the Lord one day is as a thousand years, and a thousand years as one day'.[102]

Definition

'Longsuffering is that quality of self-restraint in the face of provocation which does not hastily retaliate or promptly punish; it is the opposite of anger and is associated with mercy, and is used of God',[103] If we wish to distinguish God's longsuffering from His mercy, perhaps it could be said that mercy pities sinners in their misery, whereas longsuffering is the exercise of forbearance in the face of their defiance. Longsuffering always relates to persons and their perversity, not to things.

Some scriptural examples

The Bible supplies numerous instances of God's longsuffering. 'The Divine longsuffering waited in the days of Noah, while the ark was being prepared', 1 Pet. 3. 20. In respect of proud Pharaoh we read, 'God, wanting to show His wrath and to make His power known, endured with much longsuffering the vessels of wrath prepared for destruction', Rom. 9. 22.
Israel should have known much better, yet in the wake of the flagrant apostasy of the golden calf, God disclosed Himself to Moses as, 'The Lord, the Lord God, merciful and gracious, longsuffering, and abounding in goodness and truth',

---

[101] Ps. 103. 8, cp. 145. 8.
[102] 2 Pet. 3. 8; Ps. 90. 4.
[103] Exod. 34. 6; Rom. 2. 4; 1 Pet. 3. 20, W E VINE, *Expository Dictionary.*

43

Exod. 34. 6. The subsequent history of Israel and Judah is a sad record of provocation and backsliding.[104]

Saul of Tarsus is an outstanding example of Christ's longsuffering, 1 Cor. 15. 9. The apostle was ceaselessly amazed at the sheer wonder of it all.[105] If Christ could save a Saul, He can save anyone!

Implications

This glorious attribute of God is full of implications for our attitude and behaviour. Personally, we should maintain a profound personal appreciation of His goodness, forbearance, and longsuffering, that led us to repentance, Rom. 2. 4.

We may well ponder the enormity of the divine restraint as we contemplate the escalating wickedness of our world. Unbelief misinterprets this as indifference, but Peter warns, 'The Lord is not slack concerning His promise, as some count slackness, but is longsuffering toward us, not willing that any should perish but that all should come to repentance', 2 Pet. 3. 9. Again he counsels, 'Consider that the longsuffering of our Lord is salvation, v. 15. The sheer dimensions of God's saving purposes, beyond all human comprehension, will magnify His Name to all eternity! The Lord is certainly not slack. One day His judgement will fall, yet it remains His strange work, for He loves to save.[106] One thing is certain, the impenitent will never charge their Judge with impatience.

On the other hand, the tension between God's wrath and His restraint creates an age-long problem for the godly who suffer daily for righteousness' sake. The psalmist naturally yearns for vindication in the present, Ps. 13. However, the New Testament emboldens us to view the eternal perspective. In enduring adversity for the Lord's sake we experience fellowship with God in suffering as He bears patiently with the wicked.[107]

Our Lord's parable of the unforgiving servant, designed to teach forgiveness,

---

[104] 'Yet for many years You had patience with them, and testified against them by Your Spirit in Your prophets. Yet they would not listen; Therefore You gave them into the hand of the peoples of the lands', Neh. 9. 30.

[105] 'However, for this reason I obtained mercy, that in me first Jesus Christ might show all longsuffering, as a pattern to those who are going to believe on Him for everlasting life', 1 Tim. 1. 16.

[106] 'For the LORD will rise up . . . to do his deed – strange is his deed! and to work his work –alien is his work!', Isa. 28. 21 ESV.

[107] 2 Cor. 4. 17, 18; cp. Acts 9. 4.

serves to highlight the expected link between divine and human patience.[108] Forgiven much, how slow we in turn are to forgive, and how quickly we write people off, ct., Luke 13. 8! Let us learn well that 'love suffers long and is kind', 1 Cor. 13. 4, and part of the gracious composite fruit of the Holy Spirit is . . . longsuffering, Gal. 5. 22.

---

[108] Matt. 18. 21-35, particularly verses 26 and 29.

The Grace of God
Stuart McGahie, Tayport, Scotland

The concept of grace, often spoken of but rarely fully understood, appears almost 200 times on the pages of scripture. We often hear quick and easy definitions quoted, e.g., God's Riches At Christ's Expense – GRACE! While useful, these may distract us from understanding the true meaning and significance of grace. Its importance is imprinted loud and clear. The majority of New Testament Epistles begin and end with a declaration of the need for grace. It distinguishes the true Christian faith from all other world religions and schisms of men. Writing to Titus, Paul gives us a feel for the concept of grace, 'But after that the kindness and love of God our saviour toward man appeared . . . Not by works of righteousness which we have done', 3. 4-5. Grace is entirely undeserved on our part.

Our salvation is fully and freely provided by God in grace. The moment our eyes were opened to the work of grace, was not the moment that the work of grace began in our lives. God moved in grace before the beginning of the world, 2 Tim. 1. 9. From the first mention in scripture, 'Noah found grace in the eyes of the Lord', Gen. 6. 8, until the last, 'The grace of our Lord Jesus Christ be with you all', Rev. 22. 21, this glorious theme permeates the word of God.

Grace in Relation to God

Father – Source of all Grace

Grace is intrinsic to the character of God, and in perfect harmony with every other attribute of deity. Peter declares that God is, 'the God of all grace', 1 Pet. 5. 10. We cannot limit grace to the expression of what God does; grace is descriptive of who He is in His very essence, nature and character. When we consider the character of God, 'with whom there is no variableness, neither shadow of turning', Jas. 1. 17, we can rejoice that the grace of God is unchanging and eternal.

God is infinite, the One who is eternal, whom the heaven and heaven of heavens cannot contain. Every attribute and characteristic of God is the same, infinite in nature. Therefore, the resource of grace is unlimited, available to meet our need in every circumstance of life. Romans chapter 5 verse 20 refers to super-abounding grace, in contrast to the abounding sin within our experience. We should ever be thankful that the same super-abounding grace evident in our

47

salvation is able to sustain us throughout the trials of life. We are encouraged by the writer to the Hebrews to 'come boldly unto the throne of grace, that we may obtain mercy, and find grace to help in time of need', Heb. 4. 16. The unchanging promise of God to Paul, in his hour of need, should come with freshness to us whatever our circumstance in life, 'My grace is sufficient for you'.

God is sovereign; therefore the grace of God is sovereign. We have no claim on the grace of God, we are undeserving of the least of His mercies, and cannot in any way contribute to our standing in His presence. The wonder of grace is that despite our undeservedness, and bankrupt state before God, He still reaches out in loving kindness towards us – GRACE! How wonderful to think that this work of grace is still on-going in our lives, and will continue, 'That in the ages to come he might show the exceeding riches of his grace in his kindness towards us through Christ Jesus', Eph. 2. 7.

Christ – Revelation of all Grace (grace personified)

John reminds us that 'no man hath seen God at any time; the only begotten son . . . he hath declared him', John 1. 18. The One who is the 'Word' is the full revelation of the Father. There is nothing left unrevealed, no hidden surprises. Any limitation lies in our inability to appreciate and understand the person of Christ, and therefore God Himself. The writer to the Hebrews reminds us that He is the brightness (outshining) of His glory, while Paul, in the letter to the Ephesians chapter 1 verse 6, speaks of the glory of His grace, and John says the disciples beheld his glory, John 1. 14.

The full and complete revelation of the grace of God is found in the person of Christ. We can trace it in His momentous stoop from the realms of glory, 'For ye know the grace of our Lord Jesus Christ, that though he was rich, yet for your sakes he became poor, that ye through his poverty might be rich', 2 Cor. 8. 9. In entering into poverty, He revealed the grace of God. Philippians chapter 2 traces the downward steps of the Saviour that, for us, He might become obedient unto death, even the death of the cross.

His every word was spoken in true grace, no wonder men marvelled at 'the gracious words which proceeded out of his mouth', Luke 4. 22. The psalmist speaks of grace being poured into His lips, Ps. 45. 2. John takes us further and records Him saying, 'I have not spoken of myself; but the Father which sent me, he gave me a commandment, what I should say, and what I should speak', John 12. 49. Therefore not only the words used, but His whole manner of speech was directed of the Father – lips like lily's dropping sweet smelling myrrh.

The actions of Christ were ever in perfect harmony with His words. Not only in word, but in every aspect of His life, grace was displayed and dispensed to others.

Spirit – Spirit of Grace

The writer to the Hebrews reminds us of the Spirit of grace. Not only is the Spirit given to us in grace, but His dealings with us are further evidences of the grace of God. The spiritual gifts we are given, the ability to use them in service for God, the ability to live for God, and the freedom from the power of sin, are all evidence of the Spirit of grace indwelling us and the working out of divine purpose through us. We must always remember that for Christ to be glorified in our service, the gifts given to us in grace must be ministered to others in grace.

Relationships of Grace

Grace and Truth – The companions

We have already considered the perfect display of grace in every circumstance of the life of Christ. Wherever He went and whatever people thought of Him, He was the same. It is important to recognize that His grace was always shown while upholding all that was true. Truth and grace are the perfect companions. Grace does not set aside the requirements of God's justice or holiness, rather it satisfies them completely. To deny the truth would have been to deny Himself. In His true revelation of the Father, He revealed what it is to be holy. While He willingly veiled the outward display of His glory, holiness marked Him in every step of His pathway on earth. Exodus chapter 30 reminds us of the composition of that unique incense offered upon the golden altar. Each sweet spice was to be taken of like weight, tempered together, pure and holy. This reminds us of the perfect balance and harmony found in the person of Christ, each attribute being perfectly displayed to the glory of God.

How important it is that we seek to keep and display that perfect harmony between grace and truth. The Epistles, which present the truth and make frequent request for grace, clearly indicate that grace is essential for the outworking of truth. Likewise in our assemblies, the truth must be taught, upheld and shown in our manner of living, but let us never forget that grace is always required in the demonstration of that truth.

Grace and Law – The contrast
Paul reminds us that the purpose of the law is that 'every mouth may be stopped, and all the world may become guilty before God', Rom. 3. 19. The law, therefore, sets the standard of righteousness, and condemns even the best of men. What a contrast to the outworking of grace which is the source of righteousness, 'being justified freely by his grace', Rom. 3. 24, and offers full forgiveness to the worst of men. No wonder JOHN NEWTON wrote:

> Amazing grace, how sweet the sound,
> That saved a wretch like me.
> I once was lost but now am found,
> Was blind, but now I see.

Grace and Sin – The conqueror

We have already touched on the truth of Romans chapter 5 – 'where sin did abound, grace did much more abound'. Too often we labour under the misconception that grace is God passing over sin. The super-abounding grace of God is so much more than that. It is God meeting the demands of divine justice in the sacrificial death of His Son, that we might be freed from the dominion and penalty of sin. Romans chapter 6 verse 14 tells us that sin no longer has dominion over us, and grace has freed us from its power. However, grace is not a licence to sin; we who are now dead to sin should no longer live therein.

The greater our appreciation of the awfulness of sin and the holiness of God, the greater will be our understanding and appreciation of the grace of God. Would that each one of us would continue to grow in grace, and the knowledge of our Lord Jesus Christ as we seek to serve Him.

The Mercy of God
Steve Probert, Cardiff, Wales

The MERRIAM-WEBSTER dictionary defines 'mercy' as: compassion or forbearance shown especially to an offender or to one subject to one's power.

It is instructive that while angels are God's messengers to mankind and tell us many things about God, they never speak about the mercy of God. In scripture, we rely upon God's people to reveal something of God's mercy. They tell us that, as believers on the Lord Jesus Christ, we experience the mercy of God in two ways:

- His mercy to us as sinners
- His mercy to us as saints

We can learn much from the first occurrence of any word in the Bible, and Lot is the first person to use the word 'mercy', Gen. 19. 19. He used the word to describe the action of the two angels who were sent by God, and who physically pulled Lot out of the city of Sodom moments before it was utterly destroyed. When we, as sinners, called on the name of the Lord Jesus Christ and were saved, we also experienced the mercy of God. Our position was much more perilous than that of Lot, for being sinners we were 'offenders' towards God. We deserved eternal punishment but God showed mercy ('compassion' or 'forbearance') to us in providing a most wonderful and free salvation. Have we thanked God today for His great mercy towards us?

Speaking to Simon the Pharisee in Luke chapter 7, the Saviour used the example of two debtors: the one owed five hundred pence, and the other fifty. When the creditor frankly forgave them both, Simon rightly judged that the man with the greater debt would love the creditor most. His personal experience of the compassion and forbearance shown to him was greater, because he understood that he owed so much. The more that we recognize the sinfulness of our sin (and the overwhelming extent of our debt), the more we will love the One who showed such mercy towards us in taking that debt away from us, and nailing it to His cross.

But our experience of the mercy of God is not limited to the past, and/or the memory of our salvation from sin. Jude is the last writer in the Bible to refer to mercy. He wrote his brief letter to believers (or 'saints' – that is, those who are sanctified by God), and expressed his desire that they should keep themselves 'in the love of God, looking for the mercy of our Lord Jesus Christ unto eternal life', Jude 21. So God shows His mercy to saints as well as sinners. As before, the extent to which we appreciate this aspect of God's mercy will vary from one saint to another.

As saints living in this world we are in a dangerous environment, we are in enemy territory, for Satan is the ruler of this world, John 14. 30. We are also living in dangerous times, for Satan is the god of this age, 2 Cor. 4. 4. Without the mercy of God, the saint could not survive in such hostile conditions.

Most of us will admit that we fail our Lord from time to time; perhaps due to an attack from the adversary, but more likely because of the weakness of the flesh. As our sovereign Lord, He has the indisputable right to deal with us immediately for these failures because we are subject to His power and because, as the prophet Nathan explained to King David, our failures allow the enemies of our God to speak ill of Him, 2 Sam. 12. 14. That God does not immediately intervene in judgement and/or remove us from this scene is a sure indication of His mercy to us. Could it be that those of us who fail Him most (as believers), will come to have a deeper knowledge of God's mercy to His saints?

We may also benefit from the mercy of God in times of infirmity. Epaphroditus certainly experienced the mercy of God when he was sick unto death and God restored him to health, Phil. 2. 27. David, the sweet psalmist of Israel, tells us that God knows our bodies (our 'frame') and remembers that we are made from dust, Ps. 103. 14. In a similar vein, the writer to the Hebrews tells us that our Saviour understands our weaknesses, and is therefore able to demonstrate His compassion towards us in our infirmities. That is why he entreats us to 'come boldly unto the throne of grace, that we may obtain mercy, and find grace to help in time of need', Heb. 4. 16. If we follow his advice, we will soon discover that our God is 'full of compassion, and . . . plenteous in mercy', and, moreover, that He 'delighteth in mercy', Ps. 86. 15; Mic. 7. 18.

If this does not cause us to praise God for His great mercy to us, as sinners and as saints, we would do well to think briefly about the angels which 'kept not their first estate' and are even now 'reserved in everlasting chains under darkness unto the judgment of the great day', Jude 6. There is no mercy for them. Perhaps that is why angels never speak of the mercy of God.

The Wrath of God
Bernard Osborne, Cardiff, Wales

The Bible is absolutely clear about the reality and terror of God's wrath, in contrast to the popular objection, 'Can a loving God eternally punish anyone?' To talk of divine judgement is not very popular in this day, yet the Bible refers to it constantly. A. W. PINK wrote that 'there are more references in scripture to the anger, fury and wrath of God than there are to His love and tenderness'. God's wrath was manifested in the lives of individuals and of nations when in self-will they pursued a course of sin, injustice and impiety. In the Old Testament the destruction of Sodom and Gomorrah[109] provides an illustration of this, as does the downfall of Nineveh,[110] and the fall of Belshazzar,[111] amongst others. The emphasis is found also in the New Testament. For example, we are told, among other scriptures, that 'the wrath of God is revealed from heaven against all ungodliness and unrighteousness of men, who hold the truth in unrighteousness', Rom. 1. 18, that a person can 'treasure up wrath in the day of wrath' by impenitence and hardness of heart, Rom. 2. 5, and that salvation from wrath is available.[112] Clearly, the inspired writers had no inhibitions about declaring God's wrath. When the Bible speaks so much about it, should we be silent?

What we have to be careful of is attributing to God unworthily the feelings and passions we experience as human beings. We must on no account think of anger in God as if it were the same in all aspects as anger in man. In man, anger may be aroused by malevolent feelings towards another, or by loss of self-control, by a feeling of powerlessness in a given situation, by wounded pride, or by bad temper. This would be to misunderstand the anthropomorphic language the Bible uses of God when it employs human feelings and actions to God in order that we might understand His Person and purposes better. It is a divine condescension to our very limited ability to appreciate the greatness and Person of God. What are our weaknesses and imperfections cannot be applied to God, and the Bible takes this for granted. God does not take delight in suffering. He does not act out of irritation. His wrath is not capricious, but is always a just response to moral evil.

God's wrath is seen not only in the future; it is a present reality, Rom. 1. 18. Here we are told that it 'is revealed', and the present tense indicates that it is a present, continuous disclosure. It is against 'all ungodliness', that which blasphemes, denies, or ignores the Creator, and 'unrighteousness', that which

---

[109] Gen. 19. 23, 24.
[110] Nahum 1. 2-8.
[111] Dan. 5. 25-28.
[112] Rom. 5. 8, 9; 1 Thess. 1. 10.

wrests the claims whether of Creator, or of creature. The wrath is against those who 'suppress the truth in and by means of unrighteousness'. 'Holding down' conveys the idea of not being ignorant of the truth, but of deliberately suppressing it. That wrath is revealed in Bible history we have seen. In this chapter, Paul describes it in the phrase 'God gave them up', vv. 24, 26, 28, which is the present action of divine wrath. They had made their choice. God's wrath is something men have chosen for themselves. They chose to practise the lusts of their sinful hearts increasingly, and God gave them up to the consequences of their choice, and His decision was just.

God's wrath is always judicial, the wrath of a judge administering justice.[113] The principles of His judging are stated.[114] Unsaved sinners are described as 'by nature children of wrath',[115] that is, those who belong to wrath, who are justly under God's wrath, the antagonism of eternal holiness to sin. The law cannot help them, for it 'worketh wrath', Rom. 4. 15. The law requires perfect obedience, but it stirs up sin within men as they rebel against its commands. It causes them to transgress its commands, and the transgression provokes God's wrath. How can the sinner be delivered from the wrath which is still future, treasured up until the day of wrath, the wrath to come?[116] God has made provision in the gospel whereby sinners can cease to be the objects of His wrath, and become the recipients of His grace. On the cross the Lord Jesus Christ bore the punishment which sinners deserve, the death in their stead, and our stead, being subject to God's wrath. In this way, He became 'the deliverer from the wrath to come' to all who put their faith in Him, who 'are justified by his blood' and 'saved from wrath through him', Rom. 5. 9.

---

[113] Rom. 2. 15.
[114] Rom. 2. 2, 6, 11, 16.
[115] Eph. 2. 3.
[116] Rom. 2. 5; 1 Thess. 1. 10.

'Who for the joy that was set before him'
Ian Campbell, South Shields, England

The cross is undoubtedly the place of unparalleled sorrow. The sympathetic onlookers stood with broken hearts beholding the Just One suffering unjustly. Had not the Lord clearly indicated beforehand to his disciples that they were to 'weep and lament'? The Saviour too, according to Psalm 69, was spoken of as having a broken heart, 'reproach hath broken my heart', v. 20. One might be tempted to ask if there could possibly be any hint of joy at Golgotha that day, as the 'Man of sorrows' suffered. Surprisingly, there was, beating deep in His heart, an anticipated joy – 'Who for the joy that was set before him endured the cross', Heb. 12. 2. This immediately raises the question: 'What was that joy?'

Since the word 'joy' is singular, some might conclude that there was only *one* thing involved. However, just as the sparkling diamond is made up of many facets, we shall discover, by exploring the Epistle to the Hebrews, there were many things which, collectively, formed that singular 'joy', the joy for which He was prepared to patiently endure the agonies of the cross.

1. The cross became the altar upon which the suffering Servant offered Himself to God

The death of Christ was, first and foremost, an offering to God, 'Who through the eternal Spirit *offered himself without spot to God'*, 9. 23. On the eve of His death, though the cross lay before Him, He spoke of it as a completed work and that was a work which *glorified* God, 'I have glorified thee on the earth: I have finished the work which thou gavest me to do', John 17. 4. So delighted was God with that offering, we read, 'He shall see of the travail of his soul, and shall be satisfied', Isa. 53. 11.

2. The cross was where the will of God was carried out to the full in absolute obedience.

'Sacrifice and offering thou wouldest not, but a body hast thou prepared me . . . Then said I, Lo, I come (in the volume of the book it is written of me,) *to do thy will*, O God', Heb. 10. 5-7. At Sychar's well, He informed His puzzled disciples, 'I have meat to eat that ye know not of . . . *My meat is to do the will of him that sent me'*, John 4. 34. When saying, 'a body hast thou prepared me', the writer is quoting from Psalm 40 in the Septuagint, a Greek translation of the Hebrew scriptures. The Hebrew says, 'mine ears hast thou opened'. The ears were a most suitable symbol, as they were the organ of the reception of God's word and will. Whether we use the word 'body' or 'ear', both are fitting symbols for the

55

carrying out of God's will. 'And being found in fashion as a man, he humbled himself, and became obedient unto death, even the death of the cross', Phil. 2. 8.

3. The cross became the means whereby He would secure those He would call His brethren

'He is not ashamed to call them brethren, Saying, I will declare thy name unto my brethren, in the midst of the church will I sing praise unto thee', Heb. 2. 11-12. 'What an overwhelming truth! How humbling to have the Son of God call us brothers and not to be ashamed of it', JOHN MACARTHUR. It was imperative that He die! No cross, no brethren! 'Except a corn of wheat fall into the ground and die, it abideth alone', John 12. 24.

4. The cross became the pathway to exaltation

'Who . . . when he had by himself purged our sins, sat down on the right hand of the Majesty on high', Heb. 1. 3. This formal and dignified act of taking His seat was in response to the divine invitation, 'Sit at my right hand until I put thine enemies as footstool of thy feet', v. 13 JND. Such an invitation could be issued only upon absolute satisfaction, and it was, in itself, a declaration of the Father, 'He did always the things that pleased Me'. 'Therefore doth my Father love me, because I lay down my life', John 10. 17. The sitting down of the Son was also the positive answer to His prayer recorded in John chapter 17, 'And now glorify *me, thou* Father, along with thyself, with the glory which I had *along with thee* before the world was', v. 5 JND.

5. The cross became the means of procuring God's 'so great salvation'

'So great salvation', Heb. 2. 3. Limited by vocabulary, the writer attempts to describe what is on offer by using superlatives. Not just 'salvation'. Not just 'great salvation', but it is a 'so great salvation'. This technique is so reminiscent of Paul, when, in Colossians chapter 2 verse 9, he writes, 'For in him dwelleth all the fulness of the Godhead bodily'. Not just 'Godhead'; not just 'the fulness of the Godhead'; but '*ALL* the fulness of the Godhead bodily'.

It is a 'so great salvation' for at least four reasons:
(1) *Great because of who procured it* – The deity of Christ has been the great theme of the first chapter – 'as to the Son, Thy throne, O *God*', Heb. 1. 8.
(2) *Great because of the price that was paid* – 'How much more shall *the blood of Christ*', 9. 14.
(3) *Great because of what it saves from* – 'It is a fearful thing to fall into the hands of the living God', 10. 31.

(4) *Great because of what it procures* – 'He became the author of *eternal salvation*', 5. 9; 'having obtained *eternal redemption* for us', 9. 12.

6. The cross became the means of perfecting Christ for priesthood

'But we see Jesus . . . that he by the grace of God should taste death for every man. For it became him . . . to make the captain of their salvation perfect through sufferings', 2. 9-10.

Scripture often presents paradoxes to its reader. For example, in Luke chapter 2 verse 52, we read, 'And Jesus increased in wisdom and stature'. How can He who is God, and in whom are found all the 'treasures of wisdom', increase in wisdom? How can He who is perfect, be made perfect? 'Not that Christ needed to be made *perfect* in nature, but *perfect* in his capacity to be the Captain of our salvation, complete in all the offices which He sustains toward His redeemed people. *He must be a Sufferer that He may be a Sympathizer*; and hence His sufferings made Him perfect', CHARLES SPURGEON.

Many of the Lord's servants suffered martyrdom. Stephen was stoned to death, and Herod killed James the brother of John with the sword, but the Lord is able to sympathize with them, having passed through death Himself. 'For we have not an high priest which cannot be touched with the feeling of our infirmities; but was in all points tempted like as we are, yet without sin', 4. 15.

The story is told of a young boy, who, keen to have a puppy, responded to an advert in the local press. The farmer who was selling the pups gave him the choice of the litter, and, to his surprise, the youth chose a pup that was crippled. The farmer advised against it, saying, 'That pup will never run or jump!' The boy answered, 'Sir, that pup's going to need someone who understands him to help him along in life!' He then proceeded to pull up his right trouser leg and exposed to the farmer's view, an iron calliper and leather knee strap that supported a poor twisted leg deformed by polio! The boy was well suited to sympathize with the needs of the pup!

7. The cross allowed Him to meet the main requirement of priesthood
'For every high priest is ordained to offer gifts and sacrifices: wherefore *it is of necessity that this man have somewhat also to offer*', 8. 3. 'For every high priest . . . is ordained . . . *that he may offer* both gifts and sacrifices for sins', 5. 1.

The offering that this 'great high priest' made is a central theme of the Epistle to the Hebrews. 'So Christ was once *offered* to bear the sins of many', 9. 28. 'We are sanctified through *the offering* of the body of Jesus Christ once for all', 10.

10. 'But this man, after he had *offered* one sacrifice for sins for ever, sat down on the right hand of God', v. 12. 'For by *one offering* he hath perfected for ever them that are sanctified', v. 14.

8. The cross becomes the foundation for propitiation

'Wherefore it behoved him in all things to be made like to his brethren, that he might be a merciful and faithful high priest in things relating to God, *to make propitiation* for the sins of the people, 2. 17 JND. The backcloth of the Hebrew epistle is the Day of Atonement; this being the day in the Jewish calendar when the high priest went into the holy of holies to sprinkle the blood of the bullock and goat on and before the mercy seat, Lev. 16. The word 'propitiation' is related to the expression 'mercy seat', and is so translated by JOHN DARBY in Romans chapter 3, verse 25, 'whom God has set forth *a mercy-seat*, through faith in his blood'.

The words of ALBERT LECKIE are helpful, 'He has been "*set forth*" to view. The mercy seat was in the Old Testament hidden behind curtains but now Christ is set forth to the view of all . . . "*Propitiation*" is in fact the word for "mercy seat". This was the lid of the ark in the holiest of all. The ark contained the tables of the covenant. Cherubim looked down on the lid of the ark, which was God's throne. It only became a mercy seat when the blood of an animal, slain at the brazen altar, was sprinkled upon the throne of God. God said, "And there I will meet with thee, and I will commune with thee from above the mercy seat, from between the two cherubims which are upon the ark of the testimony", Exod. 25. 22. God meets and communes with the sinner on the ground of blood shed: this satisfies the claim of the divine throne. After the fall of man the cherubim stood between God in His righteous character and man in his guilt. In Genesis chapter 3 the cherubim wielded the flaming sword. Man could not approach God. Now, however, there are the cherubim on the throne of God and there is no flaming sword. Instead of wielding that sword to keep man out they gaze upon the blood which has satisfied the claims of God's throne enabling God to meet with man'.

'The cross is the lightning rod of grace that short-circuits God's wrath to Christ so that only the light of His love remains for believers', A. W. TOZER.

9. The cross enables Christ to bring many sons to glory

In contrast to Adam, who brought many sons to misery, the last Adam 'brings many sons unto glory', Heb. 2. 10!

In the Old Testament, the grace of God 'lifteth up the beggar from the dunghill, to set them among princes, and to make them inherit the throne of glory', 1 Sam. 2. 8. In the New Testament we discover that grace lifts the ungodly from the quagmire of sin to the glory of heaven! Immeasurable distance! The prodigal, when returning home, was content to be a mere servant, 'Make me as one of thy hired servants', Luke 15. 19, but the father would not hear of it, and he is greeted, 'This *my son'*!

The high priest on the Day of Atonement went in alone. He could not take any other person with him. In fact, scripture records, 'And there shall be no man in the tabernacle of the congregation when he goeth in to make an atonement in the holy place', Lev. 16. 17. Christ, however, is 'bringing many sons' with Him!

10. The cross opened the way into heaven

The tabernacle served as a graphic object lesson. The way into the holy of holies was blocked by 'the veil of separation'. Indeed, the injunction to Aaron was, 'that he come not at all times into the sanctuary inside the veil before the mercy-seat . . . that he die not', Lev. 16. 2. The Holy Spirit was showing 'that the way into the holiest of all was not yet made manifest', Heb. 9. 8. Access to the holy of holies was limited to the high priest to one day in the year, and when that day arrived he must enter in with the blood of the sin-offerings, the bullock and the goat. In Hebrews we learn that Christ has not entered into 'the holy places made with hands, which are the figures of the true; but into heaven itself', and He did this not with 'blood of goats and calves, but by his own blood'. The Spirit emphasizes that He did this 'once for all' and in so doing secured 'eternal redemption', ch. 9. The high priests must enter repeatedly (annually) and never secured anything of an eternal nature. The contrasts are most telling!

Even the high priest would never be marked by boldness when entering the holy of holies. His heart rate must have soared! In contrast to this, the believer is bidden to approach *with boldness* 'through the veil', and can do so with assurance and confidence because the veil has been rent 'by a new and living way', 10. 20. The word *'new'* occurs only once in the New Testament and it means 'freshly slain'. Christ, on the cross, 'freshly slain' opens the way beyond the veil into heaven itself!

11. The cross completely deals with sin

'Now once in the consummation of the ages he has been manifested for *the putting away of sin* by his sacrifice', 9. 26 JND. On the Day of Atonement the nation's sins were 'covered', for that is the meaning of the word 'atonement'. However, 'atonement' is not a New Testament word, in spite of it appearing in the King James Version, 'our Lord Jesus Christ, by whom we have now received the atonement', Rom. 5. 11. The word here is really 'reconciliation'. Christ had the joy, not of 'covering' sin, but rather 'putting it away'!

12. The cross makes forgiveness possible

'Without shedding of blood is no remission', Heb. 9. 22. The apostle Paul would also highlight this wonderful truth, 'In whom we have redemption through *his blood, the forgiveness of sins*, according to the riches of his grace', Eph. 1. 7.

13. The cross perfects the conscience

'For the law . . . can never with those sacrifices which they offered year by year continually make the comers thereunto perfect. For then would they not have ceased to be offered? Because that the worshippers once purged should have had no more *conscience of sins*', Heb. 10. 1-3. The Israelites *never* enjoyed complete rest of conscience!

'It is not that the law sacrifices *did not* perfect anyone as to the conscience, but that they *could not.* Their very repetition showed this. Could they have availed to cleanse the conscience, so that the offerer got complete relief as to the whole question of sin, they would have ceased to be offered; inasmuch as we never go on *doing* what is *done.* In point of fact their effect was in just the opposite direction. Instead of *removing* sins from the conscience as no longer to be remembered, they were formally brought to *remembrance* at least once every year', F. B. HOLE.

The believer having been 'once purged', has a conscience that can rest, 'For by one offering he hath *perfected for ever* them that are sanctified', v. 14. How this rest? 'Who shall lay anything to the charge of God's elect? It is God that justifieth . . . it is Christ that died', Rom. 8. 33-34.

14. The cross inaugurates the New Covenant

The discerning Jewish mind, when reading Jeremiah chapter 31, would have understood that God, having promised a new covenant, was making the old redundant. A simple conclusion can be drawn from this fact, 'For if that first was faultless, place had not been sought for a second', Heb. 8. 7 JND. The first was flawed! The flaw lay not in the law itself, but in those to whom it was given, 'For what the law could not do, in that it was *weak through the flesh*', Rom. 8. 3. The first covenant was brought in with blood, Exod. 24. 6-8. The New Covenant likewise must be inaugurated with blood, and that the blood of Christ. And so we read, 'the blood of the covenant, whereby he has been sanctified', Heb. 10. 29, and, 'the blood of the everlasting covenant', 13. 20.

15. The cross annuls Satan

'That through death he might destroy him that had the power of death, that is, the devil', 2. 14. KENNETH WUEST writes, 'The word "destroy" . . . means "to bring to naught, to render inoperative." Satan was not annihilated at the cross but his power was broken. Spiritual death cannot hold the person who puts his faith in the Saviour. Physical death cannot keep his body in the grave'. The Lord has entered into the strong man's house and bound him, thus rendering him 'inoperative'. His power has been 'annulled' and his goods have been plundered, Matt. 12. 29!

16. The cross becomes the supreme example of faith

'Wherefore seeing we also are compassed about with so great a cloud of witnesses . . . let us run with patience the race that is set before us, Looking unto Jesus the author and finisher of *our* faith; who for the joy that was set before him endured the cross, despising the shame', Heb. 12. 1-2.

'We have heard Hebrews chapter 11 spoken of as "the picture gallery of faith," and the opening words of the second verse of our chapter as setting before us "the great Master-piece which we find at the end of it". As we walk down the gallery we can well admire the portraits that we see, but the Master-piece puts all the others into the background. No other than JESUS is the Author – i.e., the beginner, originator, leader – and Finisher of faith. The others displayed certain features of faith; flashes of it were seen at different points of their career. In Him a full-orbed faith was seen, and seen all the time from start to finish. The little word "our" in the KJV is in italics you notice, since there is no such word in the original, and here it only obscures the sense. . . The One who was the perfect exemplification of faith is set before us as our goal, and as the Object commanding our faith. In this we have an immense advantage over all the worthies mentioned in Hebrews 11, for they lived in a day when no such Object could be known . . . here faith looks to Jesus. If He fills the vision of our souls we shall find in Him the motive energy that we need for the running of the race', F. B. HOLE.

The Lord of glory, having dismissed His spirit at 'the ninth hour', hangs limp upon the tree in a darkness that is to lift just as mysteriously as it had come. 'All the people that came together to that sight . . . smote their breasts', an act that gave expression to unimaginable sorrow! Little did they realize, the One over whom they grieved, had, in His death, secured 'the joy', a joy that, as believers, we are privileged to share. Had the Lord not intimated that this was to be so on the eve of His death? 'These things I speak in the world, that they might have *my joy* fulfilled in themselves', John 17. 13. 'Verily, verily, I say to you, that ye shall weep and lament . . . and ye will be grieved, but *your grief shall be turned to joy*', 16. 20 JND.

The Sinless Christ . . . The Impeccable Christ
Gordon Beck, Carrickfergus, Northern Ireland

The subject of our essay, which simply means, 'Christ was not able to sin', is a truth that needs to be stated firmly, for we are living in days when, in certain quarters, Christ's sinless impeccability is under severe attack. Some will know teachers both past and present, though teaching that Christ did not sin, teach that as He was human as well as divine, He could have sinned! In other words, He was not impeccable! The problem is that these teachers divide the person of Christ suggesting that as God He could not sin, but as man he could have sinned. The Lord Jesus Christ is one divine person, with two perfect natures, and what He could not do in His Godhood, He could not do in His manhood. At all times and in every circumstance of life, He was 'God manifest in flesh', 1 Tim. 3. 16.

To support the scriptural position that Christ was impeccable we will look at Christ's incarnation, a truth that has two sides. The Lord Jesus Christ is fully God and fully man.

Firstly, let us look at Him in His deity: the One who is described as the 'great God and our Saviour Jesus Christ', Titus 2. 13; the One who is the object of human and angelic worship.[117] He does what only God can do, such as the creation of the universe.[118] Again, He does what only God can do in regard to the matter of forgiveness of sin, and also the judging of men at the final judgement.[119] He is addressed in prayer.[120] He also possesses divine attributes, such as omnipresence,[121] omniscience,[122] omnipotence,[123] and immutability.[124] Further, the fullness of the Godhead dwells in Him[125] and He bears, and is given, titles that are given alone to God in the Old Testament, Isa. 44. 6; cf., Rev. 1. 17. He is the co-author of divine blessing.[126] Further, He describes angelic beings as His own.[127] In all these, we have the Lord Jesus Christ as fully God in His deity.

---

[117] Phil. 2. 9-11; Heb. 1. 6.
[118] John 1. 3; Col. 1. 16; Heb. 1. 2.
[119] Mark 2. 1-12; Col. 3. 13; John 5. 22; Acts 10. 42; 2 Thess. 1. 7-9.
[120] 1 Cor. 1. 2; 16. 22; 2 Cor. 12. 8.
[121] Heb. 1. 3; Eph. 4. 6.
[122] Rev. 2. 23.
[123] Matt. 28. 18-20.
[124] Heb. 13. 8.
[125] Col. 1. 19; 2. 9.
[126] Rev. 1. 4-5; Titus 1. 4.
[127] Matt. 13. 41.

The scriptures also speak of His humanity, 'the man Christ Jesus', 1 Tim. 2. 5, and His humanity is beautifully brought before us throughout the New Testament. In Matthew chapter 4 verse 2, we have the Lord Jesus experiencing hunger in the wilderness, and we see He knew weariness and thirst at Sychar's well.[128] He wept tears of sympathy at the death of Lazarus.[129] When we come to the Garden of Gethsemane, we see Him in agony.[130] Coming to the apex of His sufferings at the cross, He bled and died, for it is here we see the fullness of His humanity for though God cannot die, He who died on the cross was God manifest in flesh, 1 Tim. 3. 16. It is important to distinguish things which differ. Truly the hymn-writer was right in this matter when he wrote,

> 'Verily God yet became truly human –
> lower than angels – to die in our stead',
>
> H. d'A. CHAMPNEY.

And truly we can say, fully man as to His humanity in all aspects yet with one essential difference, 'sin apart', Heb. 4. 15. Peter testified to the fact that the Lord 'did no sin', 1 Pet. 2. 22, supported by the apostle Paul who states that He 'knew no sin', 2 Cor. 5. 21, confirmed by John who wrote that 'in Him is no sin', 1 John 3. 5. When the Lord Himself speaks on the subject He attests His impeccability when He challenges, 'which of you convinceth me of sin?' John 8. 46. He had a conscience that was clear of sin, 'the prince of this world cometh, and hath nothing in me', John 14. 30. Satan had no claim upon Christ, for He was impeccable; never sinned nor could sin.

Again, in Christ there was no inherent sin, 1 Pet. 1. 19. He was 'without blemish and without spot', the One who is described as 'holy, harmless, undefiled, separate from sinners', Heb. 7. 26. In all this, though truly human He was so unlike us. There was nothing within that Holy One to respond to sin, for Luke refers to Him as 'that Holy One who is to be born', Luke 1. 35 NKJV. He had no desire to engage in sin for, as the Bible shows, Christ said, 'I do always those things that please him', John 8. 29.

In conclusion, we have sought to show that the scriptures deny that Christ could have sinned, for sinful thinking and actions are absent in the Person of the Lord Jesus Christ.

---

[128] John 4. 6-7 cf., John 19. 28.
[129] John 11. 35.
[130] Luke 22. 43-46.

Christ our Saviour
Ian Affleck, Lossiemouth, Scotland

The lovely title of the Lord that we are considering in this study is that of Christ our Saviour and it is a powerful reminder to all our hearts of what the Lord Jesus did for us. He saved us from the penalty of sin and saves us from the power of sin day by day. Then, one day, He will save us from the presence of sin altogether and what a glorious day that will be! 'When He takes us by the hand and leads us through the Promised Land', it will be a land of stainless beauty and unsullied glory, even heaven itself.

We shall consider the subject under five headings:

1.   The promise of the Saviour - Acts 13. 22-23

Paul is in Antioch in Pisidia that is in Asia, preaching in a synagogue using King David as an illustration and He reminds his Jewish audience of the lovely testimony of God concerning David. God said of him:

- He is a man after mine own heart
- He shall fulfill all my will

What delight and confidence God had in David, for he had a tender yet faithful heart. But, in verse 23, Paul turns the attention of his audience to the seed of David, the long-promised Messiah, He who would be Israel's **Saviour,** even Jesus the despised Nazarene. How much more confidence would God have in great David's greater son, for He would bring even more delight to His heart. Indeed, God publicly declared, 'This is my beloved Son, in whom I am well pleased', Matt. 17. 5. Now, David did the will of God, of that there is no doubt, and he saved Israel from a life of servitude under the Philistines, when he slew their champion, Goliath of Gath, but the Lord Jesus saves from a greater foe, even Satan himself, and sin. The salvation which the Lord Jesus provides is not for the sons of Israel only but for the sinful sons of Adam's ruined race, therefore, for the whole world. John corroborates this, for, in his first epistle and in chapter 4 verse 14, we read the words, 'The Father sent the Son to be the Saviour of the world'.

2.   The provision of the Saviour - Luke 2. 11

'Unto you is born this day in the city of David a **Saviour,** which is Christ the Lord'.

What a wonderful message the angel brought to the shepherds that day. It was a message of joy and hope for all the people. The angel told of the birth of a Saviour, who would save His people from their sins, and that Saviour was for all the people. But, before He could be the Saviour, He must become a man. Therefore, in Hebrews chapter 2 verse 14 we read, 'Forasmuch then as the children are partakers of flesh and blood, he also himself likewise took part of the same'. The angel also told them of the sign by which they would know Him, 'Ye shall find the babe wrapped in swaddling clothes, lying in a manger', v. 12. What a sight to behold, Messiah, the very Son of God, not born in one of the great palaces of men nor in a home, however humble, but in the outside place, even a lowly cattle shed. The poet has penned the words so beautifully,

> Down from His glory ever living story,
> My God and Saviour came and Jesus was His name,
> Born in a manger to His own a stranger,
> A man of sorrows, tears and agonies.
> Oh, how I love Him, how I adore Him
> My breath, my sunshine, my all in all.
> The great creator became my Saviour
> And now God's fullness dwelleth in Him,
>
> WILLIAM E. BOOTH-CLIBBORN

3. The purpose concerning the Saviour - Acts 5. 30-32

Peter and John have been released from prison on condition that they would not teach in the name of Jesus and now stand accused of breaking the conditions of bail. They respond by saying, 'we ought to obey God rather than men', thus setting an example to saints of every generation. They go on to state two important facts concerning the Lord Jesus:

- The nation put Him to death, but God reversed their judgement when He raised him from the dead.
- Then God exalted Him by His power and made Him a Prince and a **Saviour** for the very people who crucified Him, so that their sins might be forgiven.

Surely, this was God's purpose in relation to the Saviour, that He would be exalted and extolled and made very high. From that high position He would be able to save to the uttermost all that come unto God by Him.

The apostles state that both they and the Spirit of God are witnesses to these things and, therefore, they will not fear what man shall do to them. Surely, they would sing the words of the old hymn, if it had been written,

I'm not ashamed to own my Lord or to defend His cause,
Maintain the honour of His word, the glory of His cross,
ISAAC WATTS

4. The prospect of the Saviour - Phil. 3. 20

'For our conversation is in heaven; from whence also we look for the **Saviour**, the Lord Jesus Christ'.

What a blessed assurance to know that the man whom this world crucified is alive in heaven today. But it is also a comfort to know that this self-same Saviour will come from Heaven to fulfill the work He has begun in every believer. To Paul, this must have been a precious truth, for he had suffered much for his faithfulness to his Saviour and I have no doubt his body was showing signs of premature ageing because of this. What joy then for Paul to look up and wait patiently for his Lord as he anticipated the wonderful change, when he would be clothed upon with a glorious body. May the prospect of the Saviour's return encourage all who know the burden of passing years and the feeble frame of mind, for He shall do what no doctor can do, that is, deliver us from the ageing process! Paul, when writing to Titus, adds another dimension to this thought when he says, 'Looking for that blessed hope, and the glorious appearing of the great God and our **Saviour** Jesus Christ', Titus 2. 13. Here the thought is not only that the Saviour is coming for His own to take them out of this world, but the fact that He is coming back to this world where He was rejected and ridiculed to set up His Kingdom. He shall reign throughout the whole world, for every knee shall bow and 'every tongue . . . confess that Jesus Christ is Lord to the glory of God the Father', Phil. 2. 11.

5. The picture of the Saviour as seen in Joseph - John 4. 42

'We believe . . . and know that this is indeed the Christ, the **Saviour** of the world'.

This was the name that Pharoah gave to Joseph after he, by his God given wisdom, made known the meaning of Pharoah's dream. By such wisdom, Joseph ensured that provision would be made against a forthcoming famine and certain death. Joseph is a lovely type of Christ the Saviour, for his way to the throne was by suffering.

Joseph was rejected by his brethren who hated him and could not speak peaceably to him. They sold him to merchantmen after having cast him into a pit and then faked his death so that their old father mourned for his son and would not be comforted. Joseph became a servant in Egypt but was falsely accused by Potiphar's wife and so was put in prison, there to await his fate. But, in the providence of God, he was brought to the palace and was made ruler throughout the land of Egypt with all being caused to bow the knee before him. This came about because Joseph was a man who brought the word of God to the people of this world and also because the Spirit of God was in him. What a fitting type of the Lord Jesus, the man of sorrows and, daily, grief's acquaintance, who came unto His own things but His own people received Him not. Men crucified Him, but God raised Him to a throne, for He not only brought the word of God to the people but He is the Word of God, the Spirit abode in Him, and He brought a greater salvation to this world than Joseph did in his day.

Is it any wonder that Mary, His mother, lifts up her heart in song and says, 'My soul doth magnify the Lord and my spirit hath rejoiced in God my **Saviour'**, Luke 1. 47. Surely, it becomes us who are saved to blend our voices with hers and, in the words of the hymn, say from the depths of redeemed hearts,

> Praise the Saviour ye who know Him
> Who can tell how much we owe Him,
> Gladly let us render to Him,
> All we are and have,

THOMAS KELLY

The Faithfulness of Christ
John Bennett, Kirkby-in-Ashfield, England

There are times when we can be fulsome in our praise and generous with our plaudits, building the reputation of men higher than we should. Scripture is much more measured in what it has to say and there are very few to whom the word 'faithful' is applied. Old Testament saints such as Abraham, Moses, David and Daniel are all called such. These were men who accomplished much for God in adverse circumstances. In the New Testament, we have Paul as he writes of Timothy, Tychicus, Epaphras, and Onesimus. However, whatever the character and achievements of these men, all were marked by failure at some stage in their lives.

Only one can carry this title of faithful to its full height. Only the Lord was perfect in every aspect of His service, unfailing in His fulfilment of all that the Father required. It is the purpose of this chapter to explore some of the features of faithfulness as displayed in the life and testimony of the Saviour and that we might also rejoice in all that means for us.

Faithful in His work for the Father

Twice in the early chapters of the book of Revelation, John acknowledges the title of the Lord Jesus as the faithful witness. [131] Of whom was the Lord a witness? In John's Gospel we read the words of the Lord to Philip, 'He that hath seen me hath seen the Father', John 14. 9. In the Lord Jesus there was one who told out the character and Person of the Father in all His fullness. If we need to know what God is like, in any particular facet of His Person, we can look to Christ who is the fullest revelation of deity. [132]

It is the writer of Hebrews who draws our attention to Christ as if to say, 'Contemplate Jesus, who is faithful'. [133] The Jewish readers of that epistle might look to Moses as the supreme example of fidelity but he cannot be compared with Christ. Only of the Lord could it be said that faithfulness was a designation of inherent character; He was faithful, He is faithful, and He will always be

---

[131] 'And from Jesus Christ, who is the faithful witness, and the first begotten of the dead, and the prince of the kings of the earth. Unto him that loved us, and washed us from our sins in his own blood', Rev. 1. 5; 'And unto the angel of the church of the Laodiceans write; These things saith the Amen, the faithful and true witness, the beginning of the creation of God', Rev. 3. 14.
[132] Cp. John 1. 18.
[133] 'Who was faithful to him that appointed him', Heb. 3. 2.

faithful! ARTHUR PINK in his commentary states, 'Faithfulness signifies two things: a trust committed, and a proper discharge of that trust'. In His prayer to the Father, the Lord could say, 'I have glorified thee on the earth: I have finished the work which thou gavest me to do', John 17. 4. This is what faithfulness really means!

There is, in the word 'witness', Rev. 1. 5, a reminder of the extent of the Lord's faithfulness. The word *martus* is also translated 'martyr', signifying one who has been prepared to give up his life in order to remain faithful. Of the extent of the Lord's faithfulness, Paul writes, 'He humbled himself, and became obedient unto death, even the death of the cross', Phil. 2. 8. The Lord knew the cost but did not shrink from paying it in order that the work of the Father might be accomplished.

'Faithful amidst unfaithfulness, midst darkness only light,
Thou didst Thy Father's Name confess, and in His will delight',
JAMES G. DECK

In the work of the Father that was accomplished on the cross by the Saviour, there was that which was necessary to 'make reconciliation for the sins of the people', Heb. 2. 17. Here is a demonstration of the Lord's faithfulness in completing the work of the Father and, also, faithfulness in offering the sacrifice that God required to deal with sin. He is 'a merciful and faithful high priest in things pertaining to God'.

But scripture indicates that there is a work that the Lord has yet to fulfil, 'And I saw heaven opened, and behold a white horse; and he that sat upon him was called Faithful and True, and in righteousness he doth judge and make war', Rev. 19. 11. As the Lord has been faithful in all that He has accomplished to date, we can be assured that judgement will fall upon the unrighteous and all rebellion will be put down. He will not fail!

Faithful in His work for us

It is also worth thinking about what the faithfulness of Christ means to us.

His Keeping Power

It is Paul who writes to the relatively young assembly at Thessalonica to say, 'Faithful is he that calleth you, who also will do it', 1 Thess. 5. 24. We need have no doubt or fear in respect to the security of our salvation. We should not focus upon the trials and difficulties of the Christian life, as real as these may be. We look to the Lord who is faithful and, as He has called us out of darkness into His marvellous light, so we can be assured He will deliver us home to glory.[134]

But what of the trials? The scriptures furnish us with many examples of those who suffered for their faith, many to death. It is not easy to remain faithful in the midst of the furnace of persecution. The example of the Lord may remain before us to encourage us but to what can we cling as we face the violence? Paul reminds the believers at Thessalonica, 'But the Lord is faithful, who shall stablish you, and keep you from evil', 2 Thess. 3. 3. We may face the wrath of 'unreasonable and wicked men', v. 2, but 'the Lord is faithful'. He is set to make us firm and to guard us. The Lord does not save us to leave us to the mercy of the evil one. In the midst of the conflict He provides the guard that will keep us. In His hands, the testimony will not fail.[135]

It is Peter who offers more practical advice, 'Wherefore let them that suffer according to the will of God commit the keeping of their souls to him in well doing, as unto a faithful Creator', 1 Pet. 4. 19. In the midst of trials we also have the resource of prayer. We can commit ourselves and the welfare of our souls to the Lord. This commitment should not be a single action but a constant attitude and is exemplified for us elsewhere in Peter's Epistle.[136] However, the apostle appeals to his readers to appreciate 'a faithful Creator'. He reminds them of One who has and continues to demonstrate His faithfulness in 'upholding all things by the word of His power'.[137] Equally, as the Creator, He knows our frame and understands all the intricacies of our beings. Perhaps Peter remembered the time when the early church faced persecution from the Jewish authorities. On that occasion, when released from prison, they gathered with fellow believers for prayer and lifted up their voices to God, 'which hast made heaven, and earth, and the sea, and all that in them is'.[138]

His Cleansing Power

One of the most vital things for any Christian is fellowship. John reminds us that 'our fellowship is with the Father, and with his Son Jesus Christ', 1 John 1. 3. However, that fellowship can be broken. It may be that the manner of our life is incompatible with our confession of faith. Do we seek the fellowship of One who is light or are we pursuing those things that pertain to the shadows? John exhorts

[134] 'Let us hold fast the profession of our faith without wavering; (for he is faithful that promised;)', Heb. 10. 23.
[135] See also 1 Cor. 10. 13.
[136] 1 Peter chapter 2 verse 23 furnishes the perfect example of what the apostle is teaching here.
[137] Heb. 1. 3.
[138] Acts 4. 23-31.

his readers that if we want the fellowship of divine Persons and the fellowship of fellow saints then we should 'walk in the light as he is in the light', v. 7. If we think of the high priest in the most holy place of the tabernacle we can get an appreciation of what it should really mean to walk in the light – the Shekinah glory of God's presence. What a responsibility is upon us! How careful we should be!

But the major barrier to fellowship is sin. John is clear in stating that although sin might not be the controlling force in our lives, it can and does intrude to damage our communion with God and fellow saints. How, then, can fellowship be restored? This is where we can rely upon the faithfulness of God in Christ, 'If we confess our sins, he is faithful and just to forgive us our sins, and to cleanse us from all unrighteousness', 1 John 1. 9. As E. W. ROGERS puts it, 'Confession is literally "speaking the same thing"; we side with God in regard to the gravity of the thing done: we do not argue or plead or excuse: we own up and make acknowledgement of guilt'.[139] In faithfulness to the work of Christ and the word of God, and on a just basis, God can and will forgive and fellowship can be restored. How precious that we can rely upon the work of Christ in salvation and in cleansing from that defilement that we contract through our movements in this scene.

As we think, then, of the faithfulness of Christ, let us remember that it is a testimony to His deity, an assurance of His finished work at Calvary, and the pledge of His ability to keep us throughout life's journey into His presence. What a truth!

---

[139] *Thoughts on the First Epistle of John*, pg. 26.

Christ Our High Priest
Brian Clatworthy, Newton Abbott, England

When we consider the work of the high priest in Israel, we immediately think of sacrifice and ritual. But, in fact, the work of the high priest began after the sacrifice had been ritually killed at the brazen altar. This prefigures the high priesthood of Christ whose intercessory work for us began after His ascension, once he had secured eternal redemption, Heb. 9. 12. As SIR ROBERT ANDERSON writes, 'And on earth it was that His *sacrificial* work in redemption was accomplished. That work, therefore, must have been complete before He entered on His High-priestly office'.[140] This is an important point since on earth Christ could not have officiated as a high priest as he belonged to the tribe of Judah not Levi, Heb. 7. 14.[141] Yet He made purification for our sins, a feat that no other high priest could accomplish, Heb. 10. 11, and then sat down on the right hand of God,[142] Ps. 110. 1; Heb. 1. 3; 8. 1; 10. 12. This is a remarkable statement because no high priest had ever sat down in the presence of God, Heb. 10. 11. What is even more significant is that Christ's present ministry for us is not associated with a material world and an earthly sanctuary, things indicative of a former covenant, Heb. 9. 1. Christ now intercedes for us in the very presence of God Himself, i.e., in the heavenly sanctuary and the true tabernacle, which God pitched and not man, Heb. 8. 2; 9. 11-12. This reflects the mediatory order of a new covenant, which crucially has been ratified by the blood of Christ, Heb. 9. 14-15. This calls for further explanation as to why a system of worship introduced by God appears to be flawed? Essentially, the question is why it was necessary then for Christ to become our high priest? A question that is interestingly anticipated for us in Hebrews chapter 7 verse 11.

This latter question can only be answered as we compare and contrast the high priesthood of Christ with that of Aaron. This is without doubt the intention of the writer to the Hebrews as he carefully constructs an argument to show how Christ not only fulfils all the requirements of the Aaronic priesthood, but surpasses it. So to prove fitness for high priesthood according to the law, i.e., the old covenant, Christ must be shown to comply with the pattern of Aaron's ministry. The writer to the Hebrews consequently provides incontrovertible proof of this in two ways. Firstly, because Aaron was human he was able to understand human frailty as he ministered before God in his capacity as a high priest, Heb. 5. 1-4.

---

[140] *Types in Hebrews*, pg. 27.
[141] But this does not mean that the form of Christ's ministry for us was not anticipated, e.g. His high priestly prayer in John chapter 17.
[142] The expression 'majesty on high' in Hebrews chapter 1 verse 3 is simply periphrasis for God.

He was taken in all his human weakness, Heb. 7. 28, to represent those who were physically alive, but spiritually dead in trespasses and sins. This did not, however, mean that Aaron was sinless, as he also had to offer sacrifices for his own sins, Heb. 5. 2-3. Hence the inherent weakness of the Aaronic priesthood! Christ, through incarnation, Heb. 2. 14-17, is likewise fitted to exercise priesthood amongst men, Heb. 5. 5, but is shown to be impervious to sin, Rom. 8. 3; Heb. 4. 15. The fact that Christ was impeccable does not mean that His temptations were unreal, Heb. 2. 18;[143] but He remained unstained by them, Heb. 4. 15, and is therefore able to provide us with sympathetic assurance when we are tempted, Heb. 2. 18; 4. 16. In contrast then to Aaron, Christ was taken from among dead men in resurrection glory to intercede for those who were once dead in trespasses and sins, but He is declared to be holy, innocent, unstained, separated from sinners, and exalted above the heavens, Heb. 7. 27 ESV.

Secondly, even though Aaron featured prominently in Israel's history, Exod. 16. 33, he did not just assume the position of high priest; he needed a definite call by God to the office, Exod. 28. 1f; Heb. 5. 4. Similarly, Christ was called of God to be a high priest, but notably His ministry is after the order of Melchizedek. Contrast the different words used for 'call' in Hebrews chapter 5. The word used in verse 4 of Aaron's call (*kalew*) merely confirms that he had been called by God. But the word used in verse 10 of Christ's call (*prosagoreuw* – a word used only once in the New Testament), can be translated as 'saluted', suggesting a public proclamation. WILLIAM LANE goes further when he states that the word conveys the idea of a formal and solemn ascription of an honorific title.[144]

In the Old Testament, leadership and high priesthood were regarded as separate functions within Israel, 2 Chr. 26. 18. Herein, then, lies the greatness of Christ's high priesthood, which is after the order of Melchizedek. He combines in His ministry both priesthood and kingship – this is foreshadowed in 2 Samuel chapter 6 when David, as king, danced before the ark wearing a linen ephod, a symbol of sacerdotal vesture.[145]

The mysterious figure of Melchizedek is only referred to in two passages in the

---

[143] 'Sympathy with the sinner in his trial does not depend on the experience of sin but on the experience of the strength of the temptation to sin which only the sinless can know in its full intensity', B. F. WESTCOTT, *The Epistle to the Hebrews*, pg. 59.

[144] *Hebrews*, pg. 110.

[145] ANDREW LINCOLN, *Hebrews – A Guide,* pg. 69, suggests that Psalm 110 verses 1, 4, contain the major theme of Hebrews – the exaltation of Christ at God's right hand, v. 1, and specifically His exaltation as priest after the order of Melchizedek according to God's oath, v. 4.

Old Testament, Gen. 14. 18-20; Ps. 110. 4, yet he also plays a significant part in our understanding of the High Priesthood of Christ as reflected in the New Testament letter to the Hebrews. Melchizedek is introduced to us when he suddenly appears to Abram, at the same time as the king of Sodom, Gen 14. 18-20. He provides refreshment to Abram and his hired servants on their return from battle. The name Melchizedek literally means 'my king is righteous', cf. Heb. 7. 2. Melchizedek is described in Genesis chapter 14 verse 18 as the king of Salem, and as being a priest of God Most High. Salem is usually understood as referring to Jerusalem, cf. Ps. 76. 3. Melchizedek is referred to on eight occasions in the letter to the Hebrews, 5. 6, 10; 6. 20; 7. 1, 10, 11, 15, 17, but no where else in the New Testament. Melchizedek's sudden appearance and then disappearance, plus the omission of any family genealogy in Genesis chapter 14, is used by the writer of Hebrews to typify the timelessness of the priesthood that resembles that of the Son of God. Melchizedek's priesthood did not depend upon succession, since there was no record of his death. Similarly, Christ's high priesthood is seen to be eternal, never to be passed to another, unlike that of Aaron who would eventually die and thereby be subject to the rules of succession, Ezra 2. 62-63; Neh. 7. 63-65. This means that Christ's ministry for us is always consistent, never subject to change or weakness, Heb. 13. 8. It has been well said that when Aaron assumed the role of a high priest, the office dignified the man. But when we think about Christ as our high priest, it is the man that dignifies the office!

We posed the question earlier as to why it was necessary for Christ to become our High Priest. The simple answer might be the failure of those who served under the old covenant to fully meet the standards and requirements of God. But, that is only part of the equation. Priestly activity under the Aaronic order was directly linked with ineffective sacrifices, Heb. 10. 1-4, so, irrespective of the value of their service, and the volume of sacrifices, they could not produce the desired effect, Heb. 10. 11. A precedent is therefore established with the priesthood of Christ in that by His one single oblation, i.e., His death on the cross, the question of sin has been dealt with once and for all, Heb. 10. 14. This now means that access into God's presence is assured for us at all times as the veil separating us from God has been removed, Heb. 10. 19-20.

We might finally ask ourselves the question 'Why then do we need a high priest under a new covenant with God?' As we have indicated previously, priesthood has to do with intercession, principally, but not exclusively, the maintenance of communion and fellowship with God. The substance of Christ's activity for us now is summarized in the table below:

Present Activity	Reference
He orchestrates the worship of God's people – the great song leader in God's presence	Heb. 2. 11-13
He continues to reconcile believers to God, because He has removed the barrier of sin thus effecting unbroken communion with God. Believers can go boldly where others were previously excluded	Heb. 2. 17; 10. 19, 21-22; 1 John. 2. 1
He provides a source of strength and encouragement to believers in times of temptation/testing, because He too has experienced severe testing/temptation	Heb. 2. 18; 4. 14-16
He ensures that our spiritual worship is acceptable to God since it is made through and by Him	1 Pet. 2. 5
Every charge/allegation brought against us on account of sin is rejected as Christ makes intercession for believers	Isa. 53. 12 Rom. 8. 33-35

We have only touched the hem of the high priest's garment, and there is so much more that could be said about Christ our high priest. Perhaps, however, the verse of an old hymn now made popular by a modern tune, will cover our inadequacy.

'Before the throne of God above
I have a strong, a perfect plea-
A great High Priest, whose name is Love,
Who ever lives and pleads for me',

C. L. BANCROFT

Christ as Judge
John Scarsbrook, Killamarsh, England

The thought of a judge or of judgement immediately brings to the minds of many the picture of a courtroom, a charge against the accused and the distinct possibility of a penal sentence. The early chapters of Paul's Epistle to the Romans present such an image, as the whole of mankind stands before the Judge of all the earth and a guilty verdict is pronounced, 'For all have sinned, and come short of the glory of God', Rom. 3. 23. While this is undoubtedly true, and an essential foundation for the doctrine developed in the epistle, the underlying presentation of divine judgement, demonstrated clearly in the Roman Epistle and throughout scripture, is not one of retributive vengeance meted out by a remote and impassive arbiter. It is rather the application of righteous justice, administered in a manner which is entirely consistent with the essential nature of a loving, merciful and longsuffering God.

God was entirely justified in His actions toward Adam and Eve when sin entered the world. His righteous character had been challenged, His veracity offended. He could have ended man's existence there and then, but instead His heart of love reached out to fallen man and the promise of a deliverer was given; One through whom salvation would be accomplished in such a way that God 'might be just', there could be no compromise of His holy character, and yet He would become 'the justifier of him which believeth in Jesus', v. 26.

As mankind multiplied, so also did their sinful ways, until the righteous judgement of the flood became inevitable. Here, also, the gracious attributes of God were seen, not only in the preservation of Noah and his family, but also in His longsuffering toward mankind as He waited while the ark was being prepared, 1 Pet. 3. 20. Later, in the days of Abraham, Sodom and Gomorrah reaped a harvest for the sin they had sown and suffered 'the vengeance of eternal fire', Jude 7, in which context Abraham declared, 'Shall not the Judge of all the earth do right?' Gen. 18. 25.

With the giving of the law a standard was set in stone for man's acceptance before God. With a detailed written code covering all aspects of life and behaviour, whether social, moral or ceremonial, provision was in place for leaders, rulers and priests to administer justice and, as necessary, sit in judgement upon their fellow men, subject, of course, to the ultimate authority of heaven. The difficulty was, however, that although the law was 'holy, and the commandment holy, and just, and good', Rom. 7. 12, obedience to its commands and absolute righteousness in its administration were impossible, because of the sinful nature of man and the weakness of the flesh', 8. 3. It required One with the authority and perfection of deity, yet, at the same time, the experiential sympathy of true humanity; Job's daysman who could put a hand upon both God and man. So, to a place and to a people prepared, 'when the fulness of the time was come, God sent forth his Son', Gal. 4. 4. He came 'in the likeness of sinful flesh', Rom. 8. 3, yet was never a partaker of Adam's fall; perfect, sinless humanity, holy, harmless, undefiled and separate from sinners, One fully qualified to judge not by appearance but according to righteous judgement, John 7. 24.

The intrinsically righteous character of the Lord Jesus was, in itself, a condemnation of those who opposed Him. Their critical spirit served only to enhance the perfection of His nature. Their cruel accusations were countered by gracious words; false allegations were met with meekness. What all but a few failed to grasp was that this first advent was essentially a mission of grace. 'I came', He would say, 'not to judge the world, but to save the world', 12. 47. Nevertheless, righteous justice must be brought to bear upon all men and, because the Lord Jesus is perfectly and uniquely fitted, He made it known that in the purposes of the Father, 'all judgment', in its administration, its severity, its sentence and reward, has been committed to the Son, 'because He is the Son of man', 5. 22, 27.

Just consider, for a moment, what mortal judge or jury could possibly make allowance for every factor, every facet and every nuance of individual human behaviour for everyone who has ever lived? Who could take into account the variations of ability and disability; intellect and ignorance; opportunity and misfortune; from the tribal people of the rain forests, the Inuit of Alaska and the desert dwellers of the world, to the global leaders in education, industry, commerce and religion? Only the One who 'needed not that any should testify of man: for he knew what was in man', 2. 25; the One 'in whom are hid all the treasures of wisdom and knowledge', Col. 2. 3. Only He can safely take responsibility for such an onerous task!

Scripture makes it abundantly clear that there is a series of events, yet future, in which the Lord Jesus will exercise His authority in the administration of righteous justice. The first of these is imminent; others will follow as the purposes of God in relation to the earth are realized. Some will be swift and brief, others over, or after, a period of time. The rapture of the church, as clearly described in 1 Thessalonians chapter 4 verses 13-18, will be followed by the unfolding plan of God, at present enshrined in prophetic scripture. Immediately, on being called from earth, believers who comprise the church will be assembled before the judgement seat of Christ, Rom. 14. 10-12; 1 Cor. 3. 12-15; 4. 5; 2 Cor. 5. 9-10. This is not a penal judgement on account of sin; for the believer, that was dealt with at Calvary. Rather, this is an assessment of service with a view to reward. As the name indicates, the judge will be the Lord Jesus and He will justly and perceptively evaluate not necessarily the volume of activity we have achieved but the value of it, not only the magnitude but more importantly the motive. With this appraisal completed, the believer can truly and fully enter into the joy of the Lord's presence and begin to appreciate the wonder of being forever with Him.

Meanwhile, back on earth, the rapture of the church has provided the catalyst for the prophetic programme to develop as outlined from Revelation chapter 6. The breaking of the seals, the blowing of trumpets and the bowls of wrath outpoured describe in graphic detail the awful devastation which will fall upon a world ripe for judgement. The specified time of tribulation will end with the return of the Lord Jesus from heaven in 'power and great glory', Matt. 24. 30; Rev. 19. 11-16. He comes not only in character as the warrior King, but also in His capacity as Judge. It would seem that Armageddon, which follows His return to earth, will be a brief encounter resulting in total defeat for the earth's armies and summary judgement visited upon the beast and false prophet, v. 20. Preparatory judgements follow to determine who will enjoy the kingdom reign which occupies so much of prophetic scripture in both Old and New Testaments. First, those of the nation of Israel, gathered from all countries wherein they had been scattered, will be brought to the wilderness border of the land and be made 'to pass under the rod', to purge out 'the rebels and them that transgress', Ezek. 20. 33-44. As a result of this judgement a regathered, restored, redeemed nation will be brought into the land promised to their forefathers.

There follows a judgement usually described as 'the judgement of the living nations', the 'sheep and goats' of Matthew chapter 25. Again, this assize, also presided over by the Lord Jesus, will apply certain criteria, particularly of behaviour toward Israel in tribulation days, to determine the occupants of the millennial earth. With Satan then bound for a thousand years, a reign of perfect righteousness is established with the Lord Jesus Himself taking the place of authority. These years will be characterized by flawless government and equitable justice. The earth, ravaged by the preceding years, will be restored and blessed, becoming abundantly fruitful.

At the end of this time, Satan will be released and, amazing as it may seem, will find an army ready to gather to his banner in opposition to the perfect administration of the Lord Jesus; proof indeed that the heart of man, even in such favourable circumstances, does not change! No battle ensues, 'fire . . . from God out of heaven' destroys the rebels and Satan is finally cast into the lake of fire, Rev. 20. 7-10.

Behold your God

One more judgement follows before the new heaven and new earth are ushered in. A great white throne is seen, apparently independent of any terrestrial foundation. Before this awesome justice bar stand 'the dead, small and great'! The books are opened, and the evidence of wasted lives and sinful works recorded; the book of life is there for inspection, bearing witness to all that their names are not recorded. This is not a trial but a sentence, all are lost. The Judge who utters the awful words once reached out and cried, 'Come unto me . . . and I will give you rest'; they refused, to their eternal loss.

The greatest blessing one can enjoy is to know the Lord Jesus as Saviour; to never live in fear of judgement on account of sin. Yet, may we ever remember to live our lives in light of that day of assessment and reward that we shall 'not be ashamed before him at his coming', 1 John 2. 28.